SO YOU FEEL STUCK IN YOUR CAREER?

20 thought-provoking ideas and 100+ self-coaching tools to awaken your inner guru and get you moving boldly!

Martha D. Karimi

ISBN: 978-9914-40-323-7

Meet the Author

Martha D.

I have spent the last twelve years recruiting and coaching high potential professionals globally to reinvent their careers. Many, if not all, are on a transitional path to new levels. They desire something more. Others are 'feeling stuck'. When we part ways, they leave feeling confident and clear on the type of career they want to build forward. They then go on to make bold moves that accelerate their aspirations. I hope this book showers you with similar transformational experiences!

I am a deep thinker. A conscious creator. And a light-hearted spirit. In this book, I fully embrace this spirit in relevance to our careers. I am aware it doesn't work for everyone, but I know it's the spirit that has helped many of my clients transform their careers. I hope you find within you a space to play along.

My career path has been filled with joyful self-experimentation. I have been a teacher, a recruiter, a coach, an entrepreneur, a management consultant, a researcher, a farm manager, a project manager, a computer assistant, an event manager, an instructional designer and now an author! I have worked for top Forbes listed companies, multi-national non-profits, start-ups and fast-growing businesses. These experiences have deepened my knowing that there is no one right path that leads to career success. We are all capable of curving our own and succeeding while at it.

In my journey, I have been blessed and found immense value from my mentors and coaches. When our mindsets shift, and we are equipped with the right tools, we can achieve anything!

When I am not transforming careers, I work as a concierge trusted advisor for forward-thinking & mission-driven organizations in Subsaharan Africa seeking their next level of growth.

And in between managing to practice yoga, meditate, read, travel and create art.

Acknowledgements

Y'all so incredible!

The divine, the supreme, the source, the higher force. For the invitation. For all the universal wisdom downloads. For the co-creation of this masterpiece.

Myself. For accepting the call. For never losing sight of the dream. For remembering and owning who I am. For the deep work through which I overcame the little lying voices that held me back from writing for over two decades. For learning to walk through each word in this book with grace.

Manuela Muller. The world is not ready for your kindness. Thank you. For patiently reading all my initial shitty drafts. For helping expand the ideas here. For putting your soul into this book.

Rhoda Omenya. You just didn't edit. I loved that you kept the readers at heart all through. Your spirit will always be a part of this gem.

Ruth Kimacia. For the excitement of being part of this project. For your patience in finding your way around my impossible design requests.

The thousands of humans with whom I have been honoured to travel this lifetime. Thank you for crossing my path. Thank you for sharing yourselves with me. Each of our encounters has planted different seeds in me that have sprouted into this book.

And to you my dear friend reading this book. For choosing to be here. For choosing to want better for yourself. For choosing the path of constant reinvention.

Contents

9 WAYS TO USE THIS BOOK IN A SMART WAY

1 Read the chapter titles. Only.

I am not kidding. Nor am I hurt. Read the headlines and ask yourself, "What can I do with this idea right now?" That is why it's a book of ideas!

2 Open any page.

Stay there until you have gained a new perspective. And then commit to acting on it immediately. Be warned: This might take from 3 minutes to several days or weeks.

3 Read it front to back.

This might take you a lifetime if you are working through the exercises.

4 Only read the stories.

They are entertaining, thought-provoking and educative.

5 Don't read the book.

Seriously, park it on your shelf and go on with life.

6 No action.

Or maybe you read the book front to back and take no action.

7 Find the highlighted self-coaching exercises.

Deeply explore these. Then read the rest of the book for fun.

8 Follow your intuition.

As you skim the table of contents, let your intuition pick the next right chapter for you! I wrote this book in a way that you can read the chapters in any order.

9 Invite a friend to read it with you.

Oh, this could be fun! Pick different chapters, work through the exercises together and share your reflections, learnings and actions you are committing to. If you do this, I would love to hear how your conversations unfold. If it's your luck-dawn, I might pop into your next meet up).

THE ORIGINS

Oh dear, where do we start?

I once facilitated a one-day career workshop for a group of professionals across different career levels. All participants were transitioning from their current employer. One participant, a 52-year-old man, shared during our closing reflection: "Wow, I don't know what to say, Martha. Today has left me feeling like everything I have known and believed about how to navigate my professional life in the last 30 years has been a lie".

My soul wept. I knew shit was real. I had to do something.

So here we are.

This book will be one heck of a ride through the snowy Himalayan mountains of Nepal, Goa's magical beaches, to the streets of high fashion in Milan. You might find my stories of growing up in Kenya intriguing.

Yes, this is a book about careers. It's a book soaked in humour, rawness and magic. We've made our professional lives too serious. It's time to unplug ourselves from this matrix that continues to steal our time and potential with a different spirit.

I am here to help you spice things up!

But...

This is also a book that requires you to do the hard work. There are no magical pills here. You will reflect on questions that no one will ever have the courage to ask you. You will challenge every belief you've ever held about what you are capable of. You will push yourself to see your career world through new lenses. In every chapter, I will invite you to experiment with the ideas and insights you gather. If you choose to commit to taking the tiny steps, the magic you seek will meet you halfway.

All in all, I hope the stories herein make you laugh. I hope they lighten up your career life. I hope you fall back in love with your incredible self.

And I hope you are transformed in ways that give you the courage to turn around and shout, "I got this", and "From here on, I am the driver of my career!"

And then go out there and take action!

Sending You Infinite Love & Light

M

GLAD YOU ARE HERE!

Hello, incredible human :)

I am delighted to begin by letting you know that…

YOU ARE NOT STUCK IN YOUR CAREER!

You are experiencing a compelling call for transformation

An invitation to plunge into what you are convinced your career should be; a thrilling adventure

A strong desire to immerse yourself in a playful & exciting game with your potential and talents

Not this mundane path you are on

This call for change, for novelty, is both urgent and enticing

It feels like a spell has been cast on you

A spell to bring you back to your place of magic

A place where you contribute and create value through your unique gifts

A place where you thrive!

You cannot resist the urge anymore

You know it's time you experienced your career life differently

Because yes

Yes you are bored sick of your current job, employer, team, etc

Nothing exciting or inspiring occurs anymore

Yes, you are wondering if this is the right career path for you

Should you drop everything and chase that venture you've been flirting with for years?

Or finally succumb to the passions that burn in your heart?

The thought of pursuing these secretly brings joys, yet you barely speak them out to the world

Yes, you are worried if such risky moves will succeed

And doubtful if your career experiences will ever get better

Yes, your current role doesn't satisfy the fantasies of your aspirations

You worry that the mirage of your ambitious goals keeps dragging further with every light of day

Yes, you are anxious about the drastically changing & unpredictable world of work

What if your profession becomes obsolete?

Yes, the global economy doesn't seem to promise better opportunities

And yes, I know on top of all this you are questioning your worth

You move through your career, wondering, am I good enough?

Am I capable of such success?

You are probably exhausted of all this

You've been hanging out in the streets of the known for so long, that you've committed your soul to your comfort zone

You snug with the familiar, but your heart longs for more

You've tried to make a few changes, only to find yourself right where you began

Maybe you've even given up on trying

"This is just how work is", you say

But YOU ARE NOT STUCK

Your whole being is Energy in Motion

Thus you can never be stuck

You've simply overextended your stay with organizations and teams that don't fan your fire

Pursuing opportunities that don't serve your true potential anymore

You've also probably been hanging out for too long with beliefs, and half-baked truths that are misleading the decisions and actions you take

And you've probably been asking yourself questions that don't bring you progressive insights

That's why change has been slow

Until this moment

When you are standing on the edge

War raging within between fear and freedom

Do I jump? Or do I keep betraying my aspirations, talents and gifts?

You are not stuck

This feeling you call stuck, is an invitation to pause

To relax a little

Take account of your career journey to-date

To acknowledge all the great things you've achieved

The goals you smashed unexpectedly

To appreciate yourself for the effort and commitment you've invested to get here

To remember those dreams that used to spark the life in you

To audit and challenge the beliefs and approaches that have shaped your career so far

To let go of what doesn't serve your progress

To forgive what holds you back

To write off the regrets that wear you down

Keeping you from moving forward

To embody new ways of being that will accelerate your aspirations

This is an invitation to take yourself less seriously

To start trusting yourself again

To pay attention to your heart, and embrace it's longings

To surrender to self-acceptance

As you plug into compassion for your flaws, scars & doubts

YOU ARE NOT STUCK

You are being called to a precious moment

A moment to reflect deeply, and see your career with new eyes

To gift yourself, the power of turning around and starting a fresh gift

This is a call for deep commitment to transform yourself, to the individual you need to be

So you can realise your next level career and life goals

My prayer is that this book becomes your trusted companion and guide, in the career revamp adventure you are about to dive into

I hope every word fills you with nothing short of joy, hope, lightheartedness and a compelling drive to act

I hope you find what it is you are seeking

From a friend you can trust

M

SET AN INTENTION

What do you desire to experience in your career as a result of reading this book?

Chapter 1

AN INVITATION TO UNSERIOUSNESS

Before work happened, we were relaxed, light-hearted beings experiencing the wonders of life. Unknowingly, as we toiled our souls away, we accumulated and passed on little traumas from awful work experiences. With time, these have moulded some of us into tense and anxious beings. And our career journeys have become unsound and distressful adventures.

It's time to stop. Stop and first acknowledge that it's unfair to keep taking ourselves so seriously in a world guaranteeing us so little. Stop and let go of the many career obligations that weigh us down. Stop and reset how we show up. So we can move through the unforeseen in gracious and buoyant ways. Stop fighting our true nature and allow light-heartedness to lead our journeys from here.

A short sweet-sour story

I met a fierce lady a few years back, somewhere along the deserted beaches of Goa. Let's call her Joy, which is more or less a true reflection of her soul. She briefly shared with me a short, sweet, and sour story of her life.

After working tirelessly for close to four decades, saving most of her earnings for a happy and long retirement, she lost it all. For a minute, I held my breath. Even with my little need for certainty, I couldn't imagine losing all my savings.

Unmoved and with a playful smile on her face, she went on to narrate. "Despite this tremendous loss, I never shed a single tear. Gaining and losing is part of life. Everything comes and goes. You can't let it get to you. So I got back on track and started all over again".

For someone who had never attended a zen meditation class, this was profound.

It was 35 degrees Celsius hot, but I was chilled to the marrow.

Joy's words recently reminded me of my mom's. Sometime back in mid-July of 2020, when everything was thick and cold. Curfews, lockdowns, more businesses were shutting down, more layoffs, more deaths, no light in sight. When it felt like most of humanity was barely holding onto the edge of a cliff. My mom called-mostly those days-to make sure I was going nowhere. In the middle of our conversation, she said, "Everything can burn down, and then you can wake up the next day and build it all again. *The most important thing right now is to make sure you are ready to start building when the morning comes.* So, stay safe. "

This time it was 13 degrees Celsius, yet these words managed to set my whole being on fire. Intellectually, I am reasonably comfortable with the idea of starting all over again. Besides, as an entrepreneur, this is a gospel you learn to live with. However, there was something strange about hearing these words afresh.

Joy went on to share her dreams of building a haven for underprivileged families in South East Asia. She was confident, just like my mom, that anything and everything could be rebuilt.

These encounters, years apart, strongly reminded me that living fully is a delicate balance between grand achievements and loss.

Dusting and lifting ourselves when we fall, keeping our chins up, our smiles real, our hearts light, and our spark fanned, no matter what.

It's undeniable that the volatile world of work can screw us badly. Yet to keep our sanity in these fleeting moments we call our lives, we must embody the fragile balance between living gracefully and sometimes painfully while never losing the ability to laugh at our lives.

And laughter, oh how we need genuine laughter in our work lives! The journey of navigating through our careers (all the decisions, moves, mistakes, luck, etc.), often with little guidance or shoulders to lean on, can be overwhelming. Along the way, we pick and carry with us painful memories of bad bosses, unfair work practices, lost opportunities, toxic work cultures, unmet goals and so on.

Cumulatively, these experiences gather in our hearts and minds, influencing how we think, feel and perceive ourselves (our potential, expertise, and worth). Eventually, shaping the decisions we take and the outcomes we achieve.

Laughter can help us lighten this unnecessary baggage that has never been ours to bear.

When we laugh, our muscles loosen up; thus, we show up for board meetings, interviews, performance and promotion conversations, and networking opportunities, relaxed.

When we laugh, we release feel-good hormones; thus, we show up for ourselves fully dressed in positive vibes, confident of our abilities to deal with anything and everything that our jobs might throw our way.

When we laugh, the production of anti-infection antibodies that protect us from infections by boosting our immunity spikes. Physical health goes a long way in boosting our work productivity and performance.

Laughter removes the psychological blocks that hold us from action and helps us win against fear and the anxieties we face daily. Laughter connects us with our inner magic and child-like wonder, a state from which anything is possible. And with our limitless potential, there is a lot that is possible. When we laugh, we activate a sense of belief and bravery within us that pumps us up to tackle the professional challenges we face.

In the early days of my career, I remember one of my supervisors who often nudged us to tap into this lightness of spirit amid our most difficult days. Our whole department would be under fire, but we would be shivering at our desks. He would walk into the office, look around at each of our stiff faces, smiling like he knew something we all didn't, and repeat for the millionth time, "Relax guys, cheer up, it's never that serious".

And immediately, something in me would shift.

I would find my breath and mysteriously gather the courage to walk through the fire. I learned to smash serious goals and overcome gruelling work and life challenges while taking myself unseriously and lightheartedly.

God knows I still take myself too seriously. Too often. More than I wish I did. It helps, though, to remember my supervisor's words. And all the remarkable goals we achieved under the magical umbrella of taking ourselves less seriously. Holding onto this memory lightens my spirit and cheats my system that everything is or will be OK. And before I know it, it is.

That is why stimulated laughter also works. Laughing is innate to us. Even if you don't feel like laughing, watch a child laugh, join a laughter yoga class, pop into a comedy improv session or stand by a group of laughing idiots, see if you resist the temptation to laugh.

Once, I had a session with a client who was at a crossroads in her career. She began by venting for 20 minutes. And then she paused and started to laugh. I couldn't resist the spontaneity, so I joined. Later, she shared she was laughing at her silliness. Through her rant, she realized that she had within her all the answers she sought to solve her career dilemma. But she had been overanalyzing each of them, and everything was muddled in her head—no wonder she was feeling paralyzed.

Instead of coaching, we each shared stories of funny career encounters. And we laughed more.

I want to believe you are an ambitious, highly self-driven ass-kicker and purpose-oriented human. You want to get there urgently. You are impatient with your current speed of growth. When any confusion or temporary challenge pops up, you feel overwhelmed by the lack of clarity. Crossroads are as frustrating as are the unwritten rules of succeeding in an unpredictable job market.

You want to get 'there', and because you are a badass, you do, only to quickly 'set new goals' for your next level. Completely missing the opportunity to acknowledge your journey so far. Fulfilment, in the long run, becomes your elusive mirage. All this feels frustrating.

When I encounter a client similar to you, I invite them to relax.

To breathe a little.

To laugh at how seriously they are taking themselves in pursuits whose outcome is out of their control.

To remember how often they have rebuilt the burnt-down houses and dreams into astonishing masterpieces.

To cast away their career doubts and worries, just for a day.

To distance their self-worth from the disruptiveness in their professional lives.

To relax and dig from their caves of forgetfulness, all the remarkable accomplishments they hoped for in the past, and have since achieved these.

To pause their taking themselves too seriously button. After all these years, if a proven formula for succeeding in our careers existed; it would be a global curriculum. Yet, I am highly doubtful if this would eliminate the suffering we experience trying to figure out all the puzzles in today's complex world.

Three hacks to unserious your career life

We know we are taking ourselves too seriously when the high expectations and standards we've set for ourselves, many of which may not be of our choosing, begin to weigh us down. In our chase to see these to light, our actions feel like a steep uphill climb. We are fighting against our true selves. Other times, we spend days beating ourselves up for the opportunities we missed or the mistakes we made. Along the way of living this way, we lose our sense of humour and are eventually in a state of despair.

You may want to pause at this moment and audit yourself. In what ways have you been taking yourself too seriously in your career journey? How do you act when you take yourself seriously? And how does this make you feel?

Furthermore, what is the impact of taking yourself too seriously all the time on your career fulfilment? And finally, how would you love to feel instead? What small actions do you need to take to embrace these new feelings?

In addition to exploring the above, take time to curiously seek to identify how you might loosen up and begin to navigate your career more joyfully and calmly through the three ideas below.

Untie yourself from obligations

What are the musts and shoulds binding you to act in particular ways and make certain decisions in your career? If you were to take an honest audit of your choices so far, how have they served you or held you back from your aspirations? Imagine living for a day without all the rules that are caging you? What would be different? What new decisions or actions would you take?

There is power in experiencing ourselves in a state opposite of what we have sentenced or accustomed ourselves to be. Are you used to taking the road on your right every evening? Why not try driving in the opposite direction and see what lies beyond your norm? Acting in unusual ways exposes us to new worlds with unique realities. These sneak previews of possibilities place in our hands the opportunity to radically and positively transform how we think, feel, and approach our career adventures.

It is also a reminder that nothing is fixed. The world overflows with multiple truths, and thus, confining ourselves within the limitations of our obligations is unfair to our potential.

We are a product of our accumulated experience. Each must and should in our lives is passed down to us, most times unknowingly. In careers, we carry a wealth of these from our past interactions with mentors, parents, role models, former bosses, friends, colleagues, acquaintances. Heck, even watching a TV series plants some shoulds and musts. All these experiences create our recipes of what we think we must follow to succeed in our careers.

Maybe you think you should pursue your Master's degree or PhD by a certain age? You must reach a particular hierarchical level in your career by a specific date. You should be earning X by (insert your unrealistic date). It would help if you did this and that, so you could achieve this and that.

There is nothing wrong with having specific standards of living. The challenge arises when we become so attached to achieving these that we forget we are operating in a world that is in a rapidly changing spiral. When our obligations that we've crowned the most important of our endeavours are unmet, we suffer.

We suffer because we've taken ourselves too seriously in the process of pursuing them. Putting all our energy and effort, even when the green lights indicate it's time to change direction. The more we fail to meet our shoulds and musts, the more we feel frustrated.

So what is the remedy? Should we stop dreaming? Of course not! Without our ambitions, we are uninspired to move.

However, ask yourself. Are these dreams and goals indeed my core aspirations? Are they authentically aligned to what I desire the most? Or have they been passed down to me throughout my life experiences? Is this what I really want for my life? Is achieving these going to make me feel genuinely happy and satisfied with my career?

While at it, it's important to reflect and take action on:

What musts and shoulds have I accumulated over the years that have become a source of constant frustration or feelings of inadequacy in my career?

What small steps can I take to explore if there are alternative realities?

How much of my sense of worth and Joy may I have attached to the achievement of these self-created expectations?

In what ways can I start to acknowledge my incredible self more often?

And in what ways can I experience more Joy and a sense of worth in my career despite the hustle and unexpected outcomes?

Bring some Wu Wei into your life

No, I don't mean stop going to work, applying for jobs, making meaningful professional connections, and instead spend your time lying around all day doing nothing, as Wu Wei is often mistaken for. Obviously, in our dream world, we all wish our career goals could miraculously be home delivered.

I recently participated in a guided walking tour in Kaya, a sacred tropical forest along the Kenyan coast. In the middle of the walk, the guide stopped abruptly. He pointed at a tree nearby and shared that it belonged to the family of strangling or killer trees. The type that thrives by growing closer to a healthy tree, feeding on it, and eventually, though not always, sucking the life out of it.

He paused and asked, "Imagine we were to initiate a forest conservation project. What do you think we should do with the strangling trees?"

I knew it was a trick question. I'm not too fond of these. I failed miserably after three trials.

"We do nothing. We let the law of nature take its course".

No cutting them down. No diverting the tree's growth aspirations.

I needed to sit still for a few minutes for this response to sink in. This type of surrender is still a stranger in my house.

The conversation reminded me of We Wui, the Chinese philosophy of 'non-doing' or 'non-action'. We Wui calls us to raise our attunement to the present, so we can flow effortlessly, act following the law of nature and, without resistance, adapt as needed. Just like kids and rivers do. Unfortunately, as we grow older, we lose track of this way of being. No wonder we move through most of our careers in a persistent resistance mode.

We resist pursuing our talents and curiosities. We resist going after the goals and dreams that call us. We resist chasing the activities that make our hearts sing. By doing so, we've put aside our true desires. This is a perfect foundation for non-ending inner fights. Surprisingly, we rarely resist the 'getting there' trap. Even though we often don't know where there is, we follow anyway. As others are moving, we move along. Eventually, we find ourselves in careers that suffocate us. When we are exhausted from swimming against the tide and breathlessly fighting against our true nature, we admit it. We feel stuck.

On the contrary, when we adopt the We Wui way, we commit to fearlessly pursuing work that utilizes our natural strengths. We know resistance will only delay our fulfilment. We sharpen our awareness to the present moment so we may catch the unforeseen shifts and spontaneous opportunities along the way.

Though we face mishaps, we do not fight them. Instead, we welcome them. Use them as opportunities to pause and discover what else we could be. Reconnect with our career aspirations. Remember what we genuinely care about. We stay with them long enough until we have spotted the hidden lessons. With this new level of knowledge, we move ahead to explore new opportunities. When we approach our careers this way, the hurdles we face feel less frictional.

So what do I do with Wu Wei?

You know all those activities in your career that make you feel like you are fighting with the current within? Yup, those, start evaluating each at a time using the questions below.

When I experience a sense of friction in any area of my career, instead of reacting in autopilot mode, what if I took a moment to reflect on:

What are the current events in my career trying to teach me?

What could be the big picture I am missing here?

How else can I flip my perception of this mess to reveal new angles and insights?

What parts of me (my strengths, talents, gifts to the world) are longing to come to life through this situation?

Integrating mindfulness practices in your life can positively influence your state of We Wui. Simple techniques like raising one's sensory awareness increase the level of attention to the unfolding life, as it is. By observing your thoughts without judgement, you become more aware of the subtle moments when resistance or unnecessary and unfruitful seriousness is arising in your career life. And from there, take action before events escalate.

Laugh at your seriousness

If you are a go-getter, you and I know we beat ourselves up too much. For the misfortunes we had no hand in, the opportunities we were not ready for, the goals we almost met, the courage we wish we could finally summon to ask for what we want. And we take many walks heavily burdened by our inaction and illusionary inadequacies. Sadly, this energy doesn't serve us.

What if we adopted the spirit of the one-year-old who sometimes bursts into laughter for no reason? What if we laughed at how silly it is to take ourselves so seriously in an unpredictable world? What if you took a moment right now to have one deep-belly laugh, letting go of the person you've been trying to be all these years? What if you laughed yourself to acceptance?

When was the last time you genuinely laughed?

Like really surrendered to the magic of free, spontaneous laughter. And let it wash away all the thoughts and emotions preventing you from tackling your challenges clear-headed?

Perhaps you can try to right now. Laugh out loud for no reason.

Really. Uncontrollably. Mindlessly. Loudly. Wholeheartedly. Honestly. Lovingly. Laughingly. Shamelessly. Fearlessly. Unrestrained. All the time, you notice yourself sinking into seriousness.

Try it right now. Till your belly and ribs bend on your knees. Let your body scream in laughter, begging you to stop. Then, laugh some more.

There is something about laughter and lightness that makes life more bearable.

Chapter 2

FROM LOCKDOWN TO LUCK-DAWN

Unpredictability can be thrilling, but it can also bring us to our knees.

Though the waves of change often bring us fortunes and gifts of limitless possibilities, they arrive disguised as trouble. In such moments, the art of asking ourselves powerful questions and adopting progressive mindsets are our necessary ingredients for unlocking new hidden opportunities. These enable us to flow smoothly with the unexpected.

Each unexpected twist and turn can be a golden opportunity to pause, carefully evaluate and critically draw the gems we need to move forward boldly.

Shit will happen anyway

If you lived through the madness that goes behind the doors of hiring processes, even for an hour, you'd relax more on taking your career too seriously. Honestly, I don't know how we professionals in the recruitment space don't have the highest rates of heart attacks.

The world of recruitment and headhunting is held together by one common thread, that anything could happen, especially the bad stuff. Half the time, we are holding our breaths, hoping for the best but expecting the worst. Will the client change the criteria in the middle of a search? Will the candidates put their best foot forward? What if the human behind this great looking resume turns out to be a terrible leader? What if candidates screw up or don't show up for interviews? By the way, on this last one, it's not cool fam. A fellow recruiter once shared with me how most of their candidates confirm to attend interviews and then don't show up.

Not that my hiring is any easier. I recruit for forward-thinking, innovative and impact-driven organisations in emerging markets. All have one thing in common; the search for superheroes who don't exist. If the client is on board with the idea that along the hiring process, shit will happen anyway, but we trust each other to figure things out, then we can partner. Acceptance and trust keeps us glued together when hit by the unexpected, which happens in every other hiring project.

Hence, when a recruiter tells you things are not always that serious, or what they seem, believe them. They are saving you a lot of drama. Believe me; they have your best interest at heart.

At some point in your career, if it hasn't happened already, shit will go down fast and hard. The unexpected will happen, and things will, for some unexplainable reasons, not go your way, no matter how hard you try. 2020 was such a year. One moment we had secure jobs, stable income, great workmates or not, but we survived. And then suddenly, out of the blues, for millions of us, what hit Joy, hit us. No memos. No warning signs. No three months prior notice.

Unless you wanted to pick a losing battle with the invincible virus, the unique angle this season brought was there was no one and nothing to blame for our losses. No bosses from hell. No unfair termination. No inhumane colleagues. Not us underperforming. No one to point fingers at. Consequently, we only had ourselves to save ourselves.

Initially, I was devastated. Like any other year, I had grand plans. It was going to be the year I finally put my foot down, set my bullshit aside, give up social media (just kidding on this one), and focus on bringing to reality the great ideas I had been grooming for years.

And then COVID-19 happened.

A few days into the madness, it dawned on me that in my decade-plus years of figuring out what the heck I am doing with my life, I have had the invaluable luxury of flexible & remote working. Surprisingly, of all my full-time jobs, only one required my physical presence. It took a global pandemic and over ten years to realise the luck I was sitting on. Does this ever happen to you? You wake up one day and realise, oh wait; I have so much I could tap into to move forward. Why was I not seeing things this way all this time?

This awareness felt like striking a gold mine. I suddenly realised that some of the remote working transitional challenges the people around me were experiencing felt like child's play for me and my team. In dismay, I watched as many business leaders flipped the pages of employment laws, unsuccessfully mining for agile answers from fixed mantras.

At some point, I got frustrated. Hence I began to channel my energy into supporting individuals and organisations to accelerate their settling down into this wholly new and somewhat scary remote working business.

Restrictive lockdowns and boredom came hand in hand for us who are energised by socialising and outdoor activities. Thus my need for adventure and diversity of pursuits was scared shitless that my life was over. Triggered by desperation, my enthusiasm spiralled. By the end of the first week, I had coined a new mission, aka survival strategy. I was committing to creating a life entertaining for myself that I would not have a single second to notice I was indoors all day, all the time.

I would turn the lockdown into fortune creation moments. Moments I came to name luck-dawns. Perhaps this way, I could manage to keep at least 1% of sanity.

Did I think it would work? Not exactly. This was one of those grand times when humanity is caught between a rock and a hard place. Externally, there were few reasons to believe in anything. But since when has that been a reason not to try?

Thus, the adventure began. First, I asked myself, "In these dark days of uncertainty, what gifts, interests and talents could I turn into fortune?" Friends have in the past labelled me as one with too many hobbies; pottery, photography, writing, reading, dancing, travelling, all things yoga related, hosting fun and enlightening experiences, music, and others I must have forgotten. Many of these would come in handy, keeping my days effortlessly activity-filled.

Two months into the lockdown, haunted by my superwoman archetype, I picked up painting. As I said, I get bored quickly. Besides, I had been curious about painting for a long time. My first trials were beautiful disasters. Now that I had all the time in the world, I could work on my craft and perhaps get good at it. Or so I thought.

One sunny Sunday afternoon, as I painted outside my house, my four neighbours' children showed up and asked whether they too could paint. By then, it was about four months since they last saw a physical classroom or left the gate. I had no reason to object.

So I gathered my four brushes, some paint, and paper and distributed them evenly. At that moment, we kicked off our twice a week painting classes. Out of the blues, COVID-19 had kicked me back to the career I had run away from years ago, teaching. Luckily, the students were better than their teacher. Often, I would be on a serious call with a client, and a child would storm into the room asking for paint.

The group grew in their consistency, and I grew remarkably in spirit. Watching their creativity skills evolve week after week, their ability to turn any idea into stunning paintings, observing them support each other genuinely and make meaning of each other's paintings, was nothing short of inspiring.

Little did I know that these moments would leave a permanent mark on my heart until several months later. In early 2021, I was having lunch at a restaurant by the Indian Ocean when a family walked in and sat nearby.

Part of the family were two lovely children who immediately grabbed their father's smartphone and started playing famous African songs. I listened, partly amused, partly nostalgic, reminiscing the moments these songs moved our world remarkably. Giving us a reason to smile amidst the darkness and unclarity of what to do with our lockdown lives-another *luck-dawn moment.*

Memories of learning certain South African dance styles from a 2-year-old boy as his friends painted came crashing on me, leaving me flooded with waves of sentiments. Call me crazy, but there were microseconds there when I suddenly & honestly missed the madness that was the year 2020.

The more the global madness unfolded, and it did turn out to be bizarre, the deeper I went into indulging from moment to moment with the question, "What in this madness could be a luck-dawn moment?" "Where in my career does the light of new revelations want to come in?" One of the ideas brought back to life then was this book.

As I held space for dozens of professionals going through similar dilemmas, I recalled a few things we take for granted or often forget, especially when things don't go our way. Going forward in this chapter, I broadly expound on three. 1) How we feel as we go through our career adventures is as important as what we do along the journey. 2) Tuning up our awareness of the world around us helps us tap 'hidden opportunities,' and 3) The quality of questions we ask ourselves is directly proportional to our achieved outcomes. Let's explore each of these further.

Your vibes are everything

You probably know this. But have you really paid attention to how your vibes affect your career progression and everyday encounters in your work?

Your vibes are your emotional state in action. Vibes are reflected by the look in your eyes, the tone and pitch of your voice, your choice of words, how relaxed or not your skin and muscles are. These physical manifestations are the reason it's hard to hide your true feelings in the presence of others.

When uncertainty visits your world of work, how you choose to respond as you steer through the changes matters. I have met far too many angry, discouraged and disgruntled humans who expect to attract new opportunities with this energy. Here is the hard truth, you will freak out the recruiter and potential employers, and they won't know what to do with you.

For me, a lockdown feel was overwhelming, frustrating, hopeless, devastating, sad, fearful, annoying, and you can go on with the list of low-frequency vibes. On the other hand, a luck-dawn feel, or rather those moments when I chose to channel fortune creation, I was optimistic, alive, brave, enthusiastic, hopeful, committed, and energised.

Every time I indulged in my work while tuned into the latter, I shocked myself with the high quality and unexpected results I generated. New ideas popped up, created alternative solutions for arising challenges and connected various ideas in interesting new ways. Anytime I tuned in to lockdown vibes, and that was a lot of time, I watched days go by, achieving little to nothing on some days.

If indeed vibes are everything, can you imagine the number of times your vibes may have influenced the opportunities you pursue? Let's say you showed up for an interview in a lockdown mood, and you sent the interviewer on a scavenger hunt trying to figure out if you are indeed such a negative-minded person?

Or let's say someone is talking to you excitedly about new career paths they came across that they think, based on your talents and interests, you could consider pursuing. And there you are, unknowingly channelling signals of disinterest at their suggestions? I mean, the opportunities could be the wrong fit for you, but a little interest to listen and acknowledge the support? Consequently, it demotivates the individual from ever sharing any opportunities with you again.

Or maybe you've accumulated years of unmet career expectations. Now you wear these as badges of resentment. Your vibes of 'it won't work' repel everyone with the slightest intention of helping you. How likely are you to attract or even notice new high-potential networks and out-of-the-box opportunities while in this energy state? Probably not much.

Luck may dawn on you unexpectedly

When the four children showed up at my doorstep, I had no idea they were angels passing by to remind me that our sense of wonder resides in us, waiting to be awakened. For over six months, they were my incredible luck-dawn.

Were they concerned about missing a whole year of school? Absolutely. As a matter of fact, they were also bored, sick and longed to reunite with their friends badly. The idea of possibly repeating the school year did not appeal to them either. Did it stop them from pursuing their daily playful adventures? Absolutely not.

A luck-dawn moment visits you in different forms and shapes. Once, I was conducting work-related research online when an advert popped up. On regular days, I quickly shut down such distractions. However, there was something uniquely different about this one. The branding captivated my attention. Intrigued, I clicked away. This move accelerated my connection to hundreds of transformational leaders and conscious communities globally. Networks that would have taken years otherwise to build.

Luck loves action. No matter how small the steps. At the moment, all I did was watch a few online videos and join a community newsletter for future updates. Silently, though, I knew I had found what I was looking for. To connect with conscious leaders with whom we inspire and challenge each other's thinking. A couple of months later, I would receive a scholarship to a global coaching program.

The unexpected just doesn't meet us. We must prepare for it, so we can recognise it when it shows up. Thus, you must always keep *your attention in the now. A moment of fortune* carries immense potential that could completely transform your career. When it arrives, your perspective shifts, and you grasp new meanings of your situation. Sometimes, several accumulated milestones collide, connecting in ways you'd never have imagined. Other times, an insight dawns on you from the blues or in a random conversation, giving you an overhaul in how you view your potential, your aspirations and the actions you are taking. You could watch something online, and suddenly your whole life is painted in front of you, making it crystal clear the steps you need to take.

Therefore, at all times, stay on the lookout for omens. These are everywhere. Often, magically masked in the mundane of everyday life. Like this other day, I struggled to celebrate completing a challenging leadership transition project I was managing. Though we were 98% done, the 2% 'not yet there' was bugging me. As I drove home that evening, I begged the universe to help me step into celebration mode. Fifty meters from my house, I spotted a lady walking by, the back of her t-shirt boldly written, 'Be Proud of Yourself'.

Why it matters to ask the right questions

The questions you ask determine the actions you take. Your actions create your life. Often, when we feel stuck, partly it's because we are asking ourselves the wrong, unthoughtful, and less impactful questions. As a result, we draw insights and make decisions that are equally underwhelming. Our questions (and the lack of them) are creating our career realities.

Powerful, well-thought-out questions might take some time to form, but they unlock the hidden fortunes in our careers when they do. We can not deny, though, that asking ourselves the *right and powerful questions* is a hard call for various reasons:

- Our ego doesn't love being challenged. The unhealthy ego receives questions as an attack.
- We love to talk about what is NOT working than we like to do something about it.

- Many of us are not exposed to cultures that allow us to question much.
- We bail on questioning our actions, events, beliefs and decisions because it is hard work.

Settling into the idea of questioning our ways is as tricky as finding the right questions to ask.

When we are ready, it is perfectly OK to take our time to find the right questions. Our patience gifts us questions that may bring the magical rapid shift we need to 'unstuck' ourselves. These periods of nonaction are not effortless. A lot is at play. Subconsciously, we are internalising and processing our journeys. Proactively, we are reflecting on the unfolding events in our careers. Periodically, we take time to critically think through each event and allow space for the dots to connect.

Unfortunately, many professionals don't have much endurance for such ways of being. Anxious to make quick shifts, they move ahead with little thought-out questions. Others voraciously search for 'how to career tips'. Seeking a one-path career formula to success in a world where everyone is figuring theirs the best way they know is deceptive.

At this point, you may realise you've already been stretching yourself by asking and allowing difficult questions. Perhaps you've had a few aha moments. Yet you are not making much progress. Then you know it's time to refine your questions!

Finding the right question/s feels like hitting the jackpot. You know, without doubt, you've found what you've been seeking. Though you've created no solutions yet, you experience a new sense of easiness and lightness. You know, by solving the arising valuable question/s, you can move forward. Everything feels right. Even if the question/s might feel somewhat uncomfortable, you know it's the first time you see your career from a completely different angle.

The better your questions get, the quicker you can pinpoint 'the root of feeling stuck' and the clearer your alternative paths of action become.

Many professionals I cross paths with mistake what finding clarity in our careers is. While they are keen to find a prescription on how to 'unstuck themselves', the truth is that clarity results from continuous reflection, patience, analysis, and taking action. Thus, this addictive pursuit of 'tell me how to', only leads one astray.

When you partner with a coach in your career reinvention journey, pay attention to the questions they pose. These are the seeds for your career transformation. Welcome the idea of dancing with thought-provoking questions. As uncomfortable as they may be, they empower you to evaluate your thinking patterns and how these shape your career realities.

Countless times, I have encountered individuals who skyrocket to senior and global roles with expansive responsibilities, just because they entertained a single uncomfortable question I threw their way in an unplanned ten minutes of catching up. A single spontaneous question became their luck-dawn moment.

Luckily, this book provides you with hundreds of questions. As you begin to welcome these into your career and craft your own, you will notice a shift in your actions, and as a result, your path starts to unfold differently.

Let's explore this mindset and technique in action.

Perhaps you feel ready for the next level in your career. You could ask yourself, "How do I move to a management role?" This question filters and limits your luck-dawn opportunities for growth to being a manager. You may be potentially allergic to management. Such roles might drown you in coordinating and overseeing teams, while what you are great at and would love to immerse yourself in is being at the front line of strategy development and driving the vision. Unfortunately, you won't know this until you are in your new 'manager' role.

Instead, you could ask, "I wonder what enhanced responsibilities I could take up to deepen my growth and tap my potential expansively ?" This question creates space for you to explore the talents, strengths, and curiosities you want to try out, thus expanding your options. The insights gained from these reflections will help you craft your ideal next-level role without being limited by standard job descriptions and titles. You may realise what you initially need is an immersion into various experiences that enable you to narrow down on roles you thrive at and align with your aspirations. This could include figuring out in risk-managed ways if being a manager is a thing for you.

Over the years, I have served hundreds of career professionals in various ways. Some through deep 1-1 coaching over an extended period, others in group career acceleration programs, and others in 15-20 minute career wake-up calls.

It's the wake-up calls that never stop to fascinate me. With only twenty minutes at hand, we dive straight into the deep end.

After a brief intro, I say,

"So (insert name). We have 15 -20 minutes together. What is the one challenge you are facing right now? "Then I pause, listen and then proceed. "What is the one question on this, if answered, you'd feel more confident to move forward and figure things out?"

The assumption is once we nail the one question, we can work through it together in the remaining or at a later time. Almost 90% of the time, we spend the first 10 minutes figuring out the challenge, not even the question. Most professionals rarely hit the nail on the head right away. While stories of their career journeys and troubles are plenty, few individuals can state what of all these, if turned upside down and inside out, would create the most significant shift in their careers. How easy is it for you to narrow down on what the issue in your career is?

Around the 12th minute of our conversation, the individual finds their aha moment (aka luck-dawn): A new way of looking at their challenges, an idea they had forgotten to act on, a realisation that they have been asking the wrong questions (common being, is it my resume?), the awareness that the ball is still in their hands and there is still a lot in their control that they have done little about, and so on.

It is worth noting that with more profound coaching sessions, we might sometimes spend two hours or longer only to get to the magical pivot point ten minutes before the end of our conversation.

Over to you: bringing luck-dawns home

Practice 1:

1) If you were to meet your future self ten years from now, what essential questions about your career growth would you be glad you asked yourself ten years back?

____

____

____

2)Among the many areas 'you feel stuck in your career', where could the idea of powerful questions shift the approaches you are using at the moment?

____

____

____

3)Later, come back to this chapter and ask yourself, 'What intriguing questions did I identify in other chapters in this book? How can these help me unlock the areas I 'feel stuck in my career?'

____

____

____

Practice 2:

1) Note down all the things you think or feel might be your career misfortunes so far. The areas where you feel stuck. Make the list as long as you can. Get creative, throw yourself one grand and final pity party. Right now.

____

____

____

2) Scan through your list once more and ask yourself: What on this list am I in control of?

____
____
____

3) What of the items I am in control of, can I take tiny actions on, starting tomorrow?

____
____
____

4) Take small steps on these and stay present to capture the outcomes of your actions. See what new ideas they reveal to you about your career, your potential, aspirations, etc.

____
____
____

Practice 3:

Reflect on: If vibes are everything, what is your career frequency?

1) How does your outlook and state of mind influence how you navigate and approach your career hurdles?

____
____
____

2) How could you be blocking yourself from accessing those unexpected pivot moments in your career?

____
____
____

3) In what ways can you start tuning up your career frequency to luck-dawn feels of joy and celebration?

Practice 4:

Moving forward. For every career decision you are about to make, ask yourself often: "What else could I be missing here?"

Consider asking your closest buddy (must be a great listener and critical thinker) to be your sounding board. Talk them through everything you've considered so far, and then ask them, "What else might I be missing here? ", "What questions have I not asked yet?"

And then listen patiently to what they create for you.

Chapter 3

TRUST YO'SELF

"As soon as you trust yourself, you will know how to live". Johann Wolfgang von Goethe.

Once, I was leading a painting class where one peculiar 9-year-old was eager to show me her new masterpiece. I stared in awe at the paper she held proudly to my face. On it, she had sprinkled thousands of colourful dots. "Wow, so many beautiful dots. Tell me more about your art piece?"

"This is a world of many people. Everyone is different, and over here I have written, that is a great thing", she replied.

In astonishment and human forgetfulness, I asked, "Hmmm, where did you learn that?"

"Nowhere, I just know it!" she replied confidently.

We are born carriers of immense wisdom, trust, faith, trust, greatness, potential, compassion, and many other positive virtues. Sadly, somewhere along the way of growing up, we forget. We forget that all the gems we need to navigate our lives lie within us.

A Rumi manifestation

Isn't it a pity that we spend most of our lives working and most of it doubting our greatness? If you choose to trust yourself a tiny bit from today, what professional opportunities would you go after?

I am confident that if you review your career history, you will find many memories of seasons when you couldn't perform plenty of complex tasks that you do today. Yet somehow, you managed to crawl yourself to mastery. You must have thought at some point, "Come on. I can do this!" or "You are better than this (insert your name)" or "I have it in me to accomplish this!"

These shots of self-belief reinforcement got you halfway there.

In this chapter, we explore how self-trust can turn around your career one decision at a time.

For the next couple of decades, the world of work will keep evolving in exciting and disruptive ways. Consequently, innumerable opportunities will arise, and many industries and jobs will transform remarkably. How will you keep up?

In times of rapid change, those who enormously believe in their abilities are courageous to play along with the unforeseen and master the art of overcoming the unexpected gracefully, who will sail less roughly. Will you be one of them?

But let's slow down a bit. Currently, as you seek to revamp your career, you will need potential employers and decision-makers to believe in you. How could that possibly happen if you don't trust in your abilities?

Suppose you have crossed paths with humans whose depth of skills and quality of results is far less than yours, their work background not as glamorous, but their level of self-belief and zeal is admirable? Maybe you've witnessed such individuals take up opportunities they are least qualified for. And when they do, they don't sit around thinking, "Oh shit, I am not good enough". Nah. They remember they have to prove themselves right, for believing in themselves. They owe themselves that. So they focus on smashing the goals at hand. They honour their self-belief.

Maybe I am a fool to believe in your potential. Or, like the 9-year-old in my painting class, I am a hopeless dreamer of a different world. A world where second-guessing our abilities every moment we need to say yes to a new challenge in our career arises less and less. A world where we trust ourselves to pursue those audacious career goals we yearn for, even when the path is unclear. A world where we wear our unique selves with a crown of pride and are unafraid to show up as we are.

The thing is, throughout my recruitment and headhunting career, I have seen and met too many non-believers. Too many humans who don't trust in their abilities even when everyone around them stands in awe of their accomplishments and potential. Great humans who I know without doubt can kick ass because, just like you, they have a track record of doing so. But then, once in a while, some little lying voice takes over, and boom, they shift into a strange, anxious, defensive and incomprehensible mode.

In psychology, they call them *triggers.*

Maybe it's a boss or a colleague or even a friend who said something two days earlier. Or their parents' voices from over two decades ago. Maybe it's one blunder in their work, in an area they are yet to master. This voice holds them hostage in the camp of "I am not good enough for this level of responsibility", "I am not ready", "I need more experience", "I should be like XYZ", "I am not capable", "I can not influence this matter", and so on. These little voices, whatever form they may take, come in between them and their Can-Do Attitude.

Over the years, it's become effortless to spot this lack of self-belief and trust in potential job candidates, especially in interview setups. Thanks to having lived through my dark days of lack of self-trust. After a long time of dancing with my belittling thoughts, I was exhausted.

Suppose I have only one thing to thank for my growing confidence and ability to smash the little lying voices. In that case, it's travelling and living abroad. Immersing in diverse cultural experiences can fill you with breathtaking, beautiful and life-transforming experiences. At first, though, the unfamiliar pisses you off by disrupting your default settings so much that sometimes you feel like you are being torn apart.

To date, 17 countries, over 50 cities across different continents and still each time I am boarding that flight, bus or ferry, I can't help but think, "What if this becomes one grand disaster?"

Beyond the hikes in dangerous terrains, being forced to alight at unsafe stops in the wee hours of the morning, shutting the heckles of 'travelling in such a country as a woman is a dangerous affair', or being caught in insane turbulences over the Mediterranean (when no one knows where the heck you are) and still finding the courage to venture into new adventures thereafter, the moments when all my "trust in yo'self Dee" and "you got this" has been called upon, is when I have travelled to non-English speaking countries. These experiences have also reinforced my belief that we are never walking alone.

Once, I was stranded for several hours (read wholly lost, confused, panicked) and unable to use physical maps that an English couple kindly gave me) in tricky corners of Siem Riep, Cambodia. Eventually, it's body language and dancing to strangers to signal I was looking for the dancing street that saved the day. From there, I found my way home. Another time I was stuck for several hours in a malfunctioned train in Poland. I urgently needed to let my friends know I had no idea when I would get home. I resorted to walking up and down the train aisle, channelling my mystical self to read each person's demeanour until I spotted a young lady who spoke English. She was kind enough to let me use her phone to contact my friends.

For a female solo traveller, these experiences can be scary at the moment. Ironically, they challenge you to build two priceless superpowers; a strong sense of calm and self-trust in any given situation.

Another superpower that comes in handy in building your self-trust is your ability to tap and use your intuition. That all intelligent and pure inner voice. Back in 2017, I vividly recall meeting an African lady from London. I was beach hopping in Goa, India. We bumped into each other at a place ladies loathe to visit in a crowded beach club, or any club really, the bathroom queue. In the mission to distract yourself from the urgency of mother nature, you can make best friends here.

Initially, she was fascinated by my hairstyle. I gave her a download of my secret, and we went back to our queuing and dancing business.

On my way out, she hurriedly came after me, obviously losing her position in the queue. At first, I thought, "How unwise". In less than 60 seconds, she was to prove me wrong. This gorgeous stranger stopped just a few inches in front of me, stared into my eyes, and said, "Everything you are seeking is within you. Trust yourself. You may have forgotten to. The gods reside within you, girl. Trust yourself". She sounded like the lady manifestation of Rumi. Then she ran back to claim her position in the queue.

Obviously, I froze. Who was this stranger channelling the 13th-century Sufi so powerfully that my world froze? I couldn't tell whether she was a psychic, an angel if I was drugged and hallucinating, or perhaps she was hitting on me. Maybe all? Maybe none? I will never know.

However, she succeeded in haunting me for the rest of my life. I have her gorgeous lovely face, her beautiful smile, her deep voice, her wild twinkling eyes stuck with me. Sometimes screaming, sometimes whispering "Trust Yourself". Especially when the little lying voices start to creep in, there she is.

You don't need to travel to build your faith in yourself. Choose to immerse yourself in spontaneous, out of your comfort and sometimes risky experiences and watch yourself rise.

Achieving high levels of confidence, trusting ourselves, self-belief, boldness or whatever you want to call it, might seem or feel like summiting Mt. Everest when you compare yourself with individuals who seem to have hacked the secret code to this way of being. Your self-belief doesn't dawn on you overnight, it unfolds over time with every small step taken. This is crucial because if you don't trust yourself in the little things, how will you trust yourself in taking giant strides?

A strong sense of awareness is vital in accelerating our self-belief. Often, we overlook the small ways we feed on the not so sacred cup of self-doubt and unnecessary worry—the accumulated impact of these speeds up the depreciation of faith in ourselves.

Begin by observing how you doubt yourself in small nonsensical things. What cardigan to buy. Should you call that person or not, and then you do. They were thinking of reaching out. Should you share that idea with your colleagues? Then you do, and it turns out to be the best idea ever. Should you send that message just the way it is? Then you do, and it turns out to be a great source of remarkable insights. Should you add that one sentence to your work presentation? And then you do, and it becomes the focal point of the whole presentation, literally stealing the show.

You will feel like a fraud, a fool, and a petrified human

Trusting yourself doesn't mean a complete absence of hesitation. On the contrary, it's your ability to acknowledge the emergence of doubt and fear and move past them that builds your self-belief.

So go on. You've been too comfortable anyways. To trust yourself is bravery. You've been wondering how you can summon courage in your career. There you have it. Trust yourself in one tiny thing.

Trusting yourself is to send second-guessing yourself and all its allies to their deathbed. Say right now, "I now choose to trust myself". Repeat it until you believe in yourself. Our lives are a result of our collective decisions. You can make this one *now, as it*'s good for your career progression and fulfilment.

It's to believe in your vision so strongly that you become unstoppable in your pursuits. It's to take the driver's seat in your career for things within your control. Trusting yourself means going ahead and making those job applications you've been eyeing and shying away from. It's to ask for that raise anyway. Confidently knowing your results speak for you.

It's to take off the mask you cling to-the mask of acceptance seeking that covers your authenticity.

To call the stranger you crossed paths with and ask to collaborate in a new venture or to volunteer in theirs. It's to believe that if other humans have done it, you are no less capable. To trust yourself is to choose the way of action. Sometimes you hear that lying voice and do it anyway. It's to raise your hand and voice an idea or concern in your next work meeting.

It's to take leaps of faith in exploring new beliefs so you can discover the version of yourself that lies on the other side. To trust yourself is to risk and own your life so that you can live fully, freely, fearlessly. Trusting yourself is to begin, now, with baby steps, and keep crawling until you can run.

> Whenever you are ready, pause and reflect.... "In what small ways, in my everyday life do I feed on the cup of self-doubt?" "Moving forward when such moments arise, what mini & counterintuitive actions can I take to move away from the hesitation so I can do what I deeply desire?"

Cut yourself loose from everything undivine

Choosing to trust yourself goes hand in hand with making difficult and unpopular decisions. This is vital, especially when we are caught up in undivine spaces that suppress our self-belief.

I know several people who quit their jobs during the global pandemic and economic downturn in 2020. Everyone thought they were crazy.

And they were.

Crazy for a better career life.

Crazy enough to believe in their potential, their values.

Crazy to believe in the abundance of the universe.

Crazy to believe they are worth more and are capable of creating remarkable results in the right work environments.

Crazy enough to trust themselves.

So they quit.

They were done.

Done with playing small.

Done with spending their time and energy pursuing visions other than their own.

Done with spending most of their jobs doing mundane work that is no reflection of their potential.

Done with ass licking terrible work environments that made them hate their actual job and dismiss their strengths.

Done waiting to start their ventures. It was time.

Done working to sustain others while their desires sat by.

Done with the stories they had been telling themselves about why they stay in their jobs.

Done worrying what others will think of them.

Done watching time pass by, slowly chipping away the enthusiasm of their aspirations.

Done waiting to take that overdue sabbatical.

Done. Done. Done.

They trusted that though this was the worst time to make such drastic decisions, there would never be a better time to make bold moves.

What seemed like drastic decisions in the eyes of others was them saying yes to novelty. Because deep down, they knew change is their cure for the fatigue of 'feeling stuck'. One single change of direction and their lives pivoted.

I know several of the same humans who are now happily engaged in new roles with incredible organizations! Indeed, we can only receive to the degree to which we are willing to let go.

So go on, cut yourself from everything undivine. Cut yourself loose from everything that depreciates your self-trust.

You can choose to begin right now.

What are the things you are holding onto in your career, yet you know too well, their time is up? They serve you no more, and only letting them go can create new spaces for something new?

List them down and begin to cut yourself loose, one undivine thing at a time. It won't be easy, but you know deep down, you can do it. And you need to. As this is your bridge to the other side of what your career might have been.

We are all winging it

You know it. I know it. We all know it.

We are all winging it.

There is no formula on 'how to make it in our careers'. This is why we need to relax. Learn to take one step at a time. Become the rule-makers. As frustrating as it is to travel in our careers without a guiding map, it's also an excellent opportunity to mould the journey into whatever we want. Johann Wolfgang von Goethe, the German poet, scientist, and theatre director, once reminded us, "Magic is believing in yourself. If you can do that, you can make anything happen". This is why I laugh when people ask how I managed to quit two jobs and make what seem like conscious decisions that have accelerated my career while I was so young. How could I have been so wise? (PS: How could I have not? Remember the 9-year-old in the chapter intro?). I laugh because, in every move in my career so far, I have been scared shitless.

Twice, I sold all my belongings to raise adequate funds to migrate to different countries to pursue a nagging career aspiration. As much as I was running away from boring jobs, I was curious to meet the human I was on the other side of fear. Trusting that I had within me the ability to traverse the consequences of what seemed like risky moves, I made several jumps towards the unknown. And this is the other thing about trusting ourselves. Deciding that no matter what the outcome, you will calmly deal with it. Because once again, you can.

This book has impacted millions of professionals globally. I am winging myself through this chapter right now. Digging deep for every wealth of knowledge in my soul has sometimes felt like a losing battle. On some 4 am writing shifts, I wonder why I chose to respond to this call. Even so, my belief in the magic that lies beyond my self-constructed limitations has seen me through. It seems somehow, as you read this, I winged myself to publishing.

An invitation to you: If you were to entertain the idea that no one knows what the heck they are doing or if it will even work out, we are all just winging. What would shift in how you navigate your career journey from here? What would you do differ

Chapter 4

STOP MAKING A LIVING. LIVE!

Most people think we are here to make a living. The truth is, we are here to live. Yup. Quote me. Thanks.

It's fascinating how busy we are. Busy pursuing work that stops our hearts from singing. Busy creating lives we don't enjoy living. We're too preoccupied with counting our paychecks to notice how quickly our lives are passing us by. So busy taking care of everyone else that we forget to take care of ourselves. Before we know it, we are unable to take care of our careers.

Why do you work so hard?

Seriously?

Have you ever pushed your limits so much in your work that you blacked out? This was me once, a few years ago. Building up to my one-month summer holiday madness across Europe, I stretched it. Literally. Worked 14 hours a day for almost three months. Yes. I am still the same mindful and conscious human you've met.

My transit in Dubai felt like one long zombie movie scene. I arrived. Slept on the floor near the boarding gate and found myself back on another flight, just in time not to starve. Somehow, making my way to my accommodation in Milan.

Then I blacked out. I slept for 12 hours non stop. No single turn. No bathroom breaks.

I was woken by the gentle touch of a middle-aged Italian lady from Siena, Tuscany. Amalia, concerned about my wellbeing, whispered in my ear until I regained consciousness. Then she offered to brew me coffee. As we sipped this strong Italian delicacy, she broke into a thousand stories about everything. Patriarchy, the Catholic church and Italy, the role of women in society, the Italian family system, spirituality - specifically, sharing about Kabbalah (a Jewish mystical religion I had recently begun studying). And then she dove straight into intergenerational family tree healing concepts.

The latter was her forte. A field she had studied and mastered while working as a waitress during the day and as a healer at night. As exhausting as this was, Amalia was committed to transitioning herself to a profession she deeply connected with. She spoke to me about how the trauma passed on to us shapes our lives. Until a family has found one individual strong enough to break the cycle by challenging their ways and or taking a different path, the path of light, the trauma keeps recurring in the family. She shared how she had courageously chosen to be the light in her family—breaking herself free and spending many years bringing the gift of healing to her community in Siena. She had fallen so deeply in love with this area that she was now studying for her bachelor's degree in the same field in Milan. Amalia had found a path worth sweat and long hours.

Before we parted ways, Amalia typed into my phone, "*Il nostro potere personale viene dalle radici. Senza radici non possiamo volare* - Our personal power comes from our roots. Without our roots, we cannot fly.

Then she was gone.

Who was this lady? Who, in a few hours, managed to transition me from my unfunctional zombie state into aliveness and wakefulness? And in doing so, giving me the most memorable and homely welcome to Italy. Her deep convictions about why she worked so hard, as well as her compelling life mission, were undeniably moving. I wanted badly to follow Amalia to her hometown. Especially since the following week was the magnificent and world's baddest horse race, Palio di Siena. If nothing else, it's because this festival was on my bucket list. And maybe I would have been initiated into the world of alternative healing modalities earlier, possibly even experienced the magic of her work.

Years later, as I explore my path in alternative healing modalities, I can't help but wonder if my journey would have accelerated if I had taken a leap of faith and said yes to her invitation. If I had not been too stuck up on my sensible 'travel itinerary'.

Among the many lessons that I carry from my powerful encounter with Amalia, of most significance is the reminder of the joy of pursuing work and interests that reflect our hearts calling.

Her efforts worked 100% in bringing me back to life after such an exhausting working season. She also planted in me an obsessive seed of reflecting on how we invest our time, energy and talents in our careers. Is it all worth it? For one to spend most of their life pursuing work they don't like. Keep themselves 'busy' so they don't face the sidelined talents that haunt them. Work tirelessly for another's vision and goals? What do we sacrifice in our lives to give our employers our all? And are these sacrifices worth the benefits we receive? Is it possible to create an alternative approach to working that doesn't consume us?

Our professions are undeniably an excellent opportunity for us to bring the best versions of ourselves to life. When this happens, we feel alive and happier. Given we spend most of our lives working, wouldn't it be exhilarating if our career encounters didn't feel like they were stealing the opportunity to live from us?

Can our careers genuinely provide us with opportunities to live fully, or if this is just a pipe dream? Let's say there is a 1% chance of such a possibility. What would it take us to realize it?

Three things have persistently stood out as I indulge in conversations with thousands of professionals about creating careers that make them feel more alive. 1) Without strong reasons for the goals we pursue, our actions may be weak or purposeless; 2) We are frequently preoccupied with activities that do not make our hearts sing, and 3) If we don't take care of ourselves, we can't take care of our careers.

Once, I led a career acceleration deep-dive masterclass with a group of ambitious and accomplished individuals from different professional backgrounds. In the room: a lawyer, a doctor, two project managers, an operations director and a marketing manager.

Many marvellous things can happen when you bring like-minded humans with diverse backgrounds into a curated safe space. Individuals in these workshops have reported feelings of boundless enthusiasm and a magical sense of self-belief. This intensified self-belief can lead to shocking insights. That's why, on this particular day, we weren't surprised when one participant said, "To be honest, after all we've covered today, I'm wondering why I go to work every day."

I watched as every other face in the room relaxed into the question. Everyone had been asking themselves the same question, but only one dared to bring up their doubts.

This is not uncommon. Rarely do we pause to ask ourselves why, apart from paying bills and following the path laid out for us, *why do we really work?* And whether these are the reasons we want to continue working for.

That powerful sharing reminded me of several other humans I have crossed paths with who have accumulated a stable source of income. Yet, they can not explain to a five-year-old why they keep up the grind.

Obviously, not everyone has such luxury. Yet, the question of why we work so hard is not reserved for the few but for us all as long as we continue to exchange our fleeting breaths for a living.

Awareness and stepping firmly into accepting why we work is the beginning of our freedom from dogmatic lifestyles. Whether that is to pay bills, earn a fortune, retire young, become an expert and a leading influencer globally in our professional field, create something magnificent, inspire a movement, leave a legacy, take care of our families, and fulfil our dreams changing the world.

Whatever it is, own it. Such clarity allows one to experience life in meaningful ways, as defined by them. When one is unsure or doesn't own why they work, they easily get caught up in the game of hiding their true intentions (which is exhausting). Or chasing goals that are out of line with their true nature (which is also exhausting).

Take a moment to reflect. What are the real reasons you work so hard? Write your first ten reasons. Then write some more. Find at least 99 reasons.

The deeper you go, the more honest with yourself you become. You will have many 'aha' moments. Some of your reasons will shock you. (Wait, what?! Really? Is that something I want? You can't imagine ever sharing some of the reasons why you work with anyone. Which is why you should find at least one person to share it with. Speaking your truth to the world helps you own it.

Once you have your list, pick any five that connect with you deeply and challenge them further:

Are these the reasons you want to continue working for? (If not, drop these and pick a new list of five. You can keep playing this way until you find 'the ones'.)

How would your career feel if you truly owned the core reasons that you are working for?

How would these reasons allow you to create more time to experience the joys of living?

Are these reasons that enable you to pursue work that allows your true self to come to life?

If they are not, what shifts need to happen?

You can keep playing with this list until you arrive at a place where you are confident you have reasons you want to continue working for.

You have one life in this physical realm, and I bet it would be more thrilling if you woke up every day, excited about the reasons you work so hard. So don't give up until you've discovered the reasons you can dance for. Strong and compelling reasons give you a handle to hang onto and steer through the hurdles and unpredictable events that unfold as you advance your career.

Enter busyness, departs living

Why are we so busy creating lives we don't enjoy living?

Several mindsets and actions have normalized busyness in our lives.

First, we have designed our lives to be full of plenty of things to do and *nothing much to be*. So little or no time to breathe and surrender to our existence. So little time to feel the life moving through and everywhere around us.

Doing nothing is a scary adventure or one that leaves us feeling guilty - for most of us. Creating spaces of solitude and nothingness requires us to face our screaming desires, untapped gifts, unmet goals, aspirations and unhealed demons. We would rather not do this. So we either label doing nothing as laziness, a vice unacceptable. Or instead, we resign to describing our days as, "I have been keeping myself busy". And eventually, our lives are lost in the only adjective that effortlessly rolls off our tongues, busy.

With every, 'I am busy' we shove aside the single most important reason we are here. To live.

Secondly, we can not imagine a life where we are disloyal to our work, our bosses, our colleagues, our family, our friends, everyone, and everything else that diverts our attention from deeply engaging with what makes us come alive, as acceptable. As a result, we give of ourselves until our cups run desert dry. This is ironic because when worst comes to worst, often the other party (such as the employer you are so faithful to) will choose what serves their most urgent and important needs. In the end, our loyalty births our distress.

Thirdly, despite us knowing our time is finite, we continue to busily pursue paths, opportunities and work activities that push us further away from what we truly want.

In my moments of existential crisis, I sometimes find myself envious of the galaxies and the coral world. They get to live for billions and millions of years as their most stunning selves. While we humans, the most intelligent of all species (assuming there were no biases in defining the scale), we are lost in busyness, putting aside our magical beingness while waiting to immerse in our joyful lives at a future time not guaranteed.

It puzzles me that we only get a short period in this thing called life and somehow manage to squander most of it successfully.

The 3-year-old purple shells collector

I met a very busy 3-year-old girl along Diani beach in Kenya a couple of months back. Actually, I didn't. I met her parents and her slightly older brother.

She didn't have time for me.

She was busy.

Busy collecting stunningly beautiful purple shells. Her eyes were glued to the sand, looking up only to add her carefully selected treasures to her mom's overflowing hands.

Before this moment, though I had been to this coastline dozens of times, I had never spotted purple snail shells.

This scene instantly tickled the child in me. My heart was star-struck at the sight of the dozen-plus shells overflowing from the little girl's mom's hands. I couldn't help myself from initiating a conversation.

"Wow, they are beautiful," I said.

"Yeah, Arti's collection," Mom responded.

Then she tried to bring my attention to little Arti.

Mom: "Arti, auntie says your shells are beautiful".

Little Girl Arti:..

Mom: "Arti, auntie says your shells are beautiful".

Little Girl Arti:..

Arti was unmoved. She went on searching for her treasure. As if nothing had transpired. As if my intrusion or her mom's words were but the crashing sounds of the ocean.

For the next one hour or so, Arti went on, deeply immersed in her task. Up and down 100 meters stretch, mom as the handler, dad and slightly older brother tagging along and me hanging around loosely. It was undeniable that we were all mesmerized.

This 3-year-old queen painstakingly picked up one purple shell at a time while quietly mumbling to herself.

Arti was busy. Busy, engaging her whole being in a task that captured all her attention, and, clearly, she loved it.

I realized then that it had been a long time since I had seen such purpose, focus, and love for a task in myself or those around me as I saw in this little girl.

Arti reminded me of the importance of pursuing work experiences and goals that deeply draw our attention, bring us joy and make us fully switched on to life. She inspired me to keep rising beyond the mundane of everyday busyness. To intentionally craft every day with activities that draw my attention and bring me joy.

A great reflection for you at this point could be:

What 'doings' are currently filling your calendar with 'busyness' but creating no magic in your life? List them, drop them one at a time.

What tiny shifts would you need to introduce to your life to bring such focus and love (like Arti's) into the work you pursue? What truly captures your attention and gets you lost in the moment? Try to immerse yourself in that more often!

The biggest joke of all time

A few years ago, I was astounded to learn that there is a day dedicated to celebrating self-care globally. It's how we react to this call of celebration that tickles and shocks me.

If we are lucky, we find out about the day from social media posts and adverts. The sight of these triggers us to make quick plans to take care of ourselves. That is if we have time. We craft lovely messages and share them with our friends and professional circles.

"Take time to celebrate yourself today". "You are important". "You matter". We hear and pass along all day. We then (again, if we have time and money) engage in activities that pamper and feed our instant gratification with a sense of self-appreciation. Only to have it all wither down before dawn.

A friend shared once that self-care for her means doing what feels right for her overall wellbeing at the moment—and taking this choice over and over again. I found this mindset profound. For most of us, most of the time, self-care remains a mirage. Once in a while, when some great force shakes us up, and we manage to look up from our busy prosaic lives momentarily, we tend to exclaim feebly, "Live a little!"

Does that mean there is something like living a lot? And if so, what is so wrong with that?

I wonder…

How can we love ourselves this way?

In my musings on the intersection of our wellbeing and career success, more questions have arisen.

How come we treat the vessel that we need to pursue our goals so unintentionally?

How come we place everyone else's interests (especially our employers' interests) before our own?

How come we shy away from celebrating our incredible selves every day?

How come we can go a day without reminding ourselves of our outstanding talents and strengths?

How come we can't spare even 60 seconds for simple pleasures like watching the sunrise or gazing at the stars?

How come we settle for below-average opportunities when we know too well our ideal job stares at us right across our desk?

How come we continue to entertain and not call out poor working conditions and manipulative bosses while our values, like freedom of expression and fairness, scream for our attention?

How can we love ourselves this way?

These questions often send me into deep, endless searches. Luckily, I am not alone. The concept of self-love and putting our needs first has existed since the 4th Century BC and was strongly advocated by the Yangists. I'm not sure how old that is, but it must have been a long, long time ago.

We are now in the 21st century, and, surprise, nothing much has changed. Doesn't the human race get tired? Will we ever learn?

Yangists saw individual wellbeing as the exclusive purpose of life. They invested all their time, effort and energy in preserving the uniqueness of individuals, protecting their nature and their wellbeing. Any action against this was declared immoral and unnecessary. Yangism encourages individuals to pursue their pleasures and desires while keeping their health safe. Consider this quote.

"What Yang Zhu was for, was the self. Even if by plucking just one hair, he might benefit the whole world, he would not do it". Mencius on Yang Zhu, Mengzi (4th century BC). Such audacity, in the middle of the ruthless warring states period, was quite brave.

Some may argue how egoistic of these men to preach so? Luckily, not much documentation is available about this philosophy to build debates around it.

But let's say we take a moment to entertain the idea of putting ourselves first: appreciating ourselves more, setting boundaries, taking our space, owning our voices, sharing our truths. Showing ourselves more compassion, embracing our uniqueness, being kind to our minds and hearts. Letting go of everything that serves us no more, cutting relationships (work or social) that make us feel less human, adopting healthier diets and walking a few miles regularly. Playing with children, dancing, taking that trip, and finally, saying no to soul-sucking work activities. Starting that hobby, doing nothing, pursuing our wildest aspirations ruthlessly, making value-driven decisions, taking that nap in the middle of the day. Owning that we matter, taking the driver's seat in our own mental and physical wellbeing, practising mindfulness, committing to inner journeys of reinventing ourselves, taking time off to refill our cups with hot chocolate...

Would we perhaps move a step closer to experiencing more fulfilment in our lives?

Choosing ourselves and our wellbeing over everything else is not an easy move. One must be convinced this is what they want to do because it serves them right.

I invite you to reflect on prioritizing yourself in your career. Referring to the self-love list shared above and adding your creative ideas:

What small ways can you choose today to start loving yourself differently? How will introducing such shifts alter how you show up and feel in your daily professional life?

Get honest with yourself. How are you currently deprioritizing taking care of yourself, including always putting your needs last? What selfish decisions do you need to make to boost your wellbeing and, ultimately, your career success?

In addition, what other new habits and mindsets do you need to a) adopt and b) let go to feel more alive?

And finally, if you ever need external help, never hesitate to seek it. As edgy as it feels, this is the ultimate expression of loving yourself!

Chapter 5

DEATH TO HUMILITY

You've been playing the career game for a while now.

What are you really proud of?

How often do you speak about it in the world? Can you say with certainty that the world knows what you are truly made of?

Does the mention of your outstanding accomplishments make you cringe?

Or maybe you sometimes belittle your magnificence so others can be seen?

Do you feel uncomfortable when you interact with individuals who are, in your opinion, less talented or less successful get ahead in their careers? When you know you are more capable? If you nodded yes to any of the above, welcome on board. This chapter will serve you well!

RIP Humility

Socrates was one of the wisest men in Athens. Today, he is recognized as one of the fathers of Western philosophy. He was a charmer whose wisdom stole the hearts and seduced the minds of many men and women from all over the Mediterranean. Interestingly, Socrates spent most of his life on one mission. To convince everyone else, he was nothing close to wise.

His deep conviction that he knew nothing propelled him to become a master of genuine inquiry. Socrates excelled at curiously guiding others in examining their ways and beliefs to achieve higher levels of understanding. In his pursuits, Socrates interviewed those who deemed themselves most discerning, often concluding they were not. Instead, he observed, it's the less notable and praiseworthy who are wiser.

He is famously quoted as, "The thing I only know is that I know nothing".

In saying so and through his actions, Socrates laid the foundation of intellectual humility. Yet, his methods led to his execution. He was accused of corrupting the minds of young Athenians.

Was his verdict reasonably justified? Perhaps this is subject to debate. Some argue that the arrogance portrayed in his defence speech led to his sentence.

Isn't it puzzling and somewhat intriguing that one could be so humble yet so defiantly arrogant?

As a talent headhunter, one is subject to collide with a wide range of humans—the highly successful and the highly arrogant. The very modest, you will sweat trying to squeeze their achievements out of them. The complacent with not much to show. The arrogant who know they are arrogant and those unaware of it. Those who play on your naivety, and so on.

In contemplating these interactions, I find myself bombarded with questions such as: "Where do we draw the line between modesty and foolish ignorance of owning our greatness?" "How does humility hold us back from our true potential?" "Does staying dumb about our achievements and letting the results speak on our behalf always serve us right?"

What does it mean in our world today to live like Socrates did, admitting not knowing? Does this serve our careers? Or betray us? Is having a high sense of appreciation for ourselves in our jobs equal to arrogance? If not, how can one maintain a high level of self-acknowledgement while, at the same time, maintaining the ability to commune with all? And in the same line of thought, when do behaviours and actions that affirm our skills and successes cross the line into arrogance? Why is it that when I acknowledge my fabulous self without hesitation, I am frequently met with statements like, "Oh, you are so full of yourself?"But I am. Full of wonder and greatness. What is wrong with acknowledging this?

Rabbit holes. In my efforts to escape from this one, I stopped and considered, "What if we removed 'humility or modesty' from our career life dictionary? How would this impact and evolve how we show up in our world of work?"

I am inviting you to join me in sending humility to rest in eternal peace. For the sake of all the bold moves ahead of you, let us ban all modest ideas and their relatives from our career lives. Let us bid farewell to everything that gets in the way of us, letting our magnificence shine.

May she, the thief of our greatness, the mask hiding our gifts, the master of shrinking our light, may she forever dance with the angels. For a long time, we've mistaken humility, and this is why we need to remember...

What practising humility in your career is NOT

My biggest worry about humility is how the idea fools us into belittling our vision, goals, and abilities. Countless times I find myself pausing professionals when they quickly drop a bombshell of an ambitious goal they just accomplished, like 'it was nothing'. Before quickly proceeding to share other matters of less significance. I invite them to pause and give themselves some credit!

Cumulatively, these 'it's nothing really' moments lead to forgetfulness of our achievements and disregard of the skills we are becoming exemplary.

In addition, every time we openly claim or silently buy into the 'I am being modest' lie, we risk our potential. The world may be in desperate need of our authentic greatness, but here we are, being humble. As a result, we are depriving ourselves and the world of our gifts.

If you are seeking new opportunities to advance your career, you can not move to greater heights while hiding your greatness.

It would help if you recognized humility for what it's not. This often unfolds in ways such as:

- Playing small
- Being unassertive in asking for what you want
- Or keeping them unmentioned, as if they were dirty little secrets
- Staying dumb in your team meetings about the phenomenal goals you recently achieved
- Feeling afraid of sharing your success. No, that is and will never be showing off
- Talking less about your ambitious 10 or 20-year goals, so others don't feel so challenged by you.
- Shrinking yourself so others can shine
- Letting others take all the glory, thinking that is what makes you a great leader
- Denying yourself opportunities by letting others pursue what you desire
- Using phrases such as 'We did it' all the time as if you had no significant role to play
- Choosing not to mention your unique ways of contribution
- Letting modesty keep your mouth shut when you know you are the only human in the room who is 100% correct

These and all other ways of thinking or acting that minimize or conceal your true abilities and accomplishments are worth leaving behind. They deprive you of the joy and fulfilment that arises when one immerses in pursuing what makes them come alive.

The behaviours and attitudes you may be confusing with humility fall under the arrogance bucket. You know, stuff like this:

- A self-inflated ego
- Looking down upon others' accomplishments
- Looking down upon others' shortcomings
- Rudeness to your colleagues
- Undervaluing another's work output and effort
- Not preparing for an interview or a performance review, assuming that others should just know how great you are.
- Treating others as unworthy
- Inconsiderate behaviours and actions at work
- Language that belittles interviewers
- Lack of interest or show of care for fellow humans at work
- Pursuit of activities that safeguard only our interests at the cost of others
- Lack of genuine interest in the ideas or opinions expressed by others (colleagues, potential employers, etc.)

Such actions denigrate the humanness, abilities, and successes of others. In doing so, it fuels the toxic workplaces that we are all running away from.

I now pronounce you a bragger

What in your career are you really proud of? Can you say with certainty that the world knows what you are truly made of?

Do you recall those moments when you patted your back and felt amazingly good afterwards? Didn't you wish you could do this more often? You even made a promise to but never honoured it. You are not alone.

A few months ago, someone asked, "Martha, you have such a remarkable career (I wasn't feeling it, but I guess I do). How often do you pause to acknowledge yourself? In fact, why don't you share what you've accomplished thus far in your career?" Of course, my mind went blank.

We get so immersed in our day-to-day hustle that we barely take time to pause, look up and admire the wonderful things we have created. This question made me feel both uncomfortable and sad. I know I have created some incredible results over the years. How can I barely recall any at the snap of a finger? If I am not proud of my outstanding accomplishments, why am I doing all this in the first place? Of course, such questions didn't make it easier. I wanted to run. This person, on the other hand, was adamant. I took a deep breath and started recounting the big and small milestones in my journey so far. Strangely, as soon as I settled into speaking them out and allowing myself to feel a deep sense of self-appreciation, my list overflowed. An hour later, I couldn't stop myself!

When I was done, I noticed my heart felt lighter, and I was more in touch with my talents and expertise. I was even experiencing a renewed sense of confidence! I was astonished that I was the same human behind all those incredible things I had just shared!

After that mind-blowing self-appreciation encounter, I started a new acknowledgement practice. Every Friday, at 6 pm, for 30 minutes, I would sit quietly and list all the things I was proud of accomplishing that week. The more I practised, the more my confidence grew. Several weeks later, I thought about passing on this magic with one of my communities. In the back of my mind, I foolishly believed that it would be easier to remember the things I was proud of this time. After all, I had been practising, right? I was blank for the initial ten minutes.

Celebrating, acknowledging ourselves, appreciating our sense of wonder, our gifts, our bravery, and everything that makes us outstanding is something we know we should do. Still, often we are unable to step into that space within us that allows us to. And even when we do, it's temporary, and we are quick to stop. Somewhere along the way, we learnt that admiring our spectacle is unacceptable.

While this occurs for different reasons, the common trend is that we are afraid. We fear that sharing our successes sets new bars we must reach, which poses a risk of being judged harshly in the future, should we achieve less. Others see speaking about their accomplishments as a curse on their future success. While for some of us, we are afraid we may lose our circles when we stand out. Moreover, in most societies, acknowledging ourselves is looked down upon and misinterpreted as boasting or arrogance. Thus, we feel guilty when we act or behave in any manner that puts our accomplishments out there.

On the contrary, as we've earlier seen, there is a significant distinction between what humility in your career is not and what arrogance is. And, of course, walking around all day, every day, talking excessively about your achievements, might turn out to be a source of misery for the people around you. It's polite to be mindful that others might not be in the energy space to take in all your achievements all the time.

Why does it matter that we get comfortable with acknowledging our successes? When you connect with potential employers or collaborators, they want to know what you're made of right away. And to be honest, many of us recruiters are bored, impatient and just hanging around for someone to spark our imagination. We hire them, and we move on to new, exciting projects. Furthermore, interviewers and potential hiring managers have limited time. They also lack magical powers to figure out your most significant career milestones unless you directly, openly and compellingly share them.

Openly communicating our accomplishments is a way of owning them and demonstrating the value we can create. It also increases our confidence and happiness.

An invitation at this moment to pause and reflect:

How would you feel if you started acknowledging yourself publicly more than you currently do?

How would you move through your career adventures if you allowed yourself to own your goodness, gifts, successes, and uniqueness and articulate them fearlessly and proudly?

Imagine yourself freely and boldly owning the human you are. Free to speak of your greatness authentically, all the time. See yourself being comfortable sharing about the great projects you recently delivered and how your unique skills and attributes saved the day. See yourself acknowledging your achievements without any fear of judgment or being misunderstood. Without a doubt, you know you have accomplished all these amazing things because that is who you are. An outstanding individual capable of producing exceptional results. You are simply letting the world know who you are and what you are made of. How would you feel being part of such a world?

Your 60-day path to bragging

So if it's not bragging but letting the world know who you are and what you are capable of, why are we using the word in the first place? Great question. So you can get over it.

Right now, your list of things to brag about might be blank. You may be wondering if you've done anything lately that you are proud of. You may even have forgotten the last big goal you achieved.

A day in your life can sometimes feel like a lifetime, thanks to the many hats you juggle. Multiple complex projects while collaborating with leaders from diverse backgrounds. Fire fighting while pursuing new opportunities and pushing through your newly launched projects. Coaching your team. And let's not even get started with managing your personal life. Recalling what you achieved an hour ago might sometimes feel like an elusive chase: so many moving pieces, so little time to breathe. Furthermore, with our brains processing over 2500 thoughts an hour, remembering our successes cannot be left to chance.

Begin by setting your intention to commit to a practice of self-acknowledgement. Then create space and time to immerse yourself in sweet reminders of your magnificent self. Here you review, reflect and update your latest achievements. The more you dedicate yourself to this space, the more your successes become alive in you.

As a result, it's easier for you to remember your achievements in the heat of the moment, making you look good when you need to.

When a recruiter or potential hiring manager asks for the proudest moments in your career, you need to instantly tune into your awesomeness and share the best version of yourself. The experiences that are a true reflection of your capabilities. Nothing hurts more than knowing you undersold yourself in hiring conversations because, well, you forgot.

Frequency kills forgetfulness. Begin right now.

Block 30 minutes every end of the week. Stretch it if you wish. Call it bragging time, the hour of honour, proud of me time, the godly half hour, my badassery remembrance hour, keeping my greatness in check. Call it anything you want that brings your mind and heart to a state of appreciation and celebration. Because that's what bragging is really about. Recognizing and celebrating our career achievements. Tiny and grand, continuously.

During your remembrance hour, be sure you are in a quiet place that allows you to be still. Pause and ask yourself:

"What are the two or three things I'm most proud of having accomplished this week?"

Or if you like, add some spice for enthusiasm's sake -

"What 2-3 things did I smash like the pro I am this week? And while I was at it, I felt like the superhuman that I am?"

Alternatively, "What action did I take this week that made me feel like the badass I am?"

"'How did it feel to accomplish this?

"What did these accomplishments teach me about my abilities?"

To capture the true essence of your achievements and your magic ingredients for success, I recommend using the PAR approach. This approach helps you organize and share your experiences in a concrete, systematic, data-backed and compelling manner.

What the heck is the PAR approach?

Problem: State the work PROBLEM situation that needed to be addressed.

Action: State the strategic ACTION or APPROACHES you initiated or executed to solve the specific problem

Results: State the immediate and long-term RESULTS / IMPACT achieved in your work, team and organization.

Once you get into the rhythm of this weekly practice, you will start to remember previous accomplishments, sometimes from 5 or more years back. Savour the moments and record them for future reference.

Additionally, you will start to realize that your tiny weekly accomplishments are not so tiny after all in the grand scheme of things. You will begin to see yourself differently in your glory. When that happens, thank me wherever you are. Oops, did that make you cringe? I know I am full of myself. Complete with immense and unique value that the world needs. And so do you!

Finally, the grand idea behind documenting your accomplishments is to bring to your attention the patterns of your strengths and talents. This awareness feeds into how you communicate your worth in interviews, internal promotions or performance review conversations that you often dread because you don't have much to say.

Eventually, thanks to your long list of successes, you will have curated a valuable resource that displays your exceptional self. This is your guide to making conscious career decisions.

Chapter 6

EXPERIMENT EXPERIMENT EXPERIMENT!

Somewhere between the current state of your career and your aspirations is a **garden of** possibilities waiting to be explored.

Becoming a passionate and strategic experimenter who leaves no talents, interests and curiosities untapped is your ticket to maximising these possibilities, living your potential fully and landing those incredible opportunities you seek.

Making Trial & Error Your Path to Success

$P(A) = P(A \cap B) + P(A \cap Bc)$

You are probably wondering, "What the heck does Math have to do with my career?"

Everything.

Now, I would love to engage in an intellectual conversation about the above formula, but I beg to take a bow. Math has never been my forte. Nonetheless, a few math concepts fascinate me and are highly relevant to our daily lives.

I am referring to the law of probability, which explores the likelihood of specific events taking place. The law is split into three; the law of addition, the law of multiplication, and the law of large numbers. In the context of our careers, we will be exploring the latter.

This law states that the more you try something, the closer you get to the probability that you want to. This includes performing random trials repeatedly and failing frequently. It's like playing dice. Now, the rest of it is a bit complicated for my brain, so let's leave it at that for now.

Bringing the law of large numbers home - the more experimental you are with your career, the faster your chances of discovering where your sweet spot (strengths, spark, talents, gifts, what you do best, passion, etc.) lies. Additionally, the higher your likelihood of getting the opportunities you desire.

Now you may wonder, "Why would I want to invest my time and energy in trials that guarantee me no success?" Great question.

Firstly, for obvious reasons, nothing in life is guaranteed, especially in our careers. Besides that, our generation will shift professions three or four times in our lifetimes.

Secondly, suppose you've had ambitious career aspirations that haven't seen the light of day. In that case, this is an idea worth your attention. Perhaps you've convinced yourself you have insufficient time to pursue these goals or are waiting for 'the perfect conditions (that never show up) to get started.

Cultivating a practice of intentionally trying out different interests and aspirations in small doses cumulatively builds your muscles and momentum to take on bigger goals. With each win, you learn, your worries and fears slowly chip away, boosting your confidence to boldly make the moves you wish to.

Thirdly, perhaps you've fallen into the trap of sole dedication to one career path despite all signs in your industry or occupation pointing towards potential significant changes. You are hopeful of a better future, you say. This reminds me of a time on the Phi Phi Islands when we sailed into a storm despite being warned (multiple times) about possible weather changes later in the day. Although we survived the rough Andaman sea, the journey back was too scary to be worth the risk. We could have listened. We could have started our journey back earlier. We could have taken a different route. We could have taken any of the other several (and safer) adventure options. There is so much more we could have considered doing. But we chose not to.

If any of the above rings a bell, you should read the rest of this chapter. But before we move ahead, take a deep breath and, as you exhale, ditch the idea of having a well-defined, glorious career path as your recipe for success. Let go of the fixed mindset that there is only one specific career destination meant for you. Remember, your potential is infinite; hence, you could end up in many different places in your career and still be happy and fulfilled. The invitation here is to welcome into your life a more playful, trial and error and yet highly strategic approach to navigating your career growth journey. One allows you to quickly learn and filter your focus areas while you confidently drop what's not working. As a result, accelerating the pace at which you achieve your goals.

The plans and approaches you've taken in the past have only led you so far, and now you thirst for novelty. A new way that helps you unpuzzle this game in your professional life is this.

If you look closely, you'll notice that the best days at work are usually when something unusual and unexpected happens. You can't wait to get home and exclaim, "Oh my, something so interesting happened at work today!" You'd love to see the same element of inspiring surprises in your career. What a delight it would be for you to proclaim often, "Oh my, so many incredibly exciting events are unfolding in my career!"

This yearning for something different. This envy when you see others experiencing thrilling careers. This burning itch to touch something outside your mundane professional life. Something that lights your spark. This prayer you have offered or hope you have held on, that one day you will finally find the bravery to dip your feet into those things you've been curious about all these years. This hanker finds a job you are passionate about and engages in work that triggers your sweet spot. Work that enables you to bring your magic into the process of creating extraordinary results.

This is your invitation to start experimenting!

Surprisingly, though we long for new experiences, many of us remain fearful of the unfamiliar. Leaping into our interests, choosing unlikely career paths, making uncommon decisions or simply putting one of our talents out there to see where we end up, is foreign grounds for many professionals. Despite these being the likely actions to lead us to what we truly desire, we hang back and eventually do nothing. It's understandable. We have fed our mantra of 'what if we fail' so remarkably well that we've killed our experimental and playful nature. In doing so, we've let our true nature, where only learning and discovery lie, wither.

This struggle between the desire versus our well-fed fearful mantra creates a state of constant inner battle that keeps us right where we are in our careers. In this chapter, we explore: How might we find the courage to unplug ourselves from this state of inaction so that we can pursue what we crave in our careers?

As the world of work remains unforgivably erratic, professionals are pushed to make drastic moves anyway to stay relevant, competitive and somehow future-proof. Thus, developing experimental mindsets and approaches in our careers is not a luxury but a mandatory ingredient for success. To secure our future, we must prepare for the unknown.

The various ideas, talents, skills, interests and strengths that we've allowed to lay low must be put to the test so we can unleash new opportunities and possibilities for growth in an uncertain job market.

Our experimental approaches will differ depending on our circumstances. While some may have the luxury of leaving their jobs to explore new opportunities for a year or more, others may need to devise creative ways to explore new opportunities and interests while remaining in their regular jobs.

Moreover, as we run our career experiments, moving through our decisions with intention is key. Some people follow their urges and change jobs, employers and careers rapidly, only to later realise that the clarity and fulfilment they seek remains elusive. When this happens, it's easy to find fault with the external world for making them 'have to move'. To these people, I pose the challenge: Are you jumping or are you experimenting?

To experiment or not?

I once encountered a professional who had worked for 15 years in the same organisation that guaranteed her job security and competitive compensation. For the previous five of the fifteen years, the organisation had undergone significant changes. Initially, gradually and then rapidly due to various market trends. Though all the omens were clear that her role would soon be declared redundant, she hung around.

She needed help. She shared that she wanted to change, learn something new, anything that *would keep her busy (Danger alert)*. I was surprised at how little thought she had put into the kind of learning and support that would bring her the most significant shift.

Her circumstances demanded a more proactive, fast-paced and self-driven approach. Yet, she thought taking another 'professional course' (whose specifics were still unclear) was what would get her into a more exciting and stable role. Though she felt stuck, she strangely didn't seem to have the sense of urgency to make even a single disruptive move.

For such an individual, it's sad to think that, while experimentation is their best bet for reinvention, it will take forever for them to warm up to the idea. Unfortunately, when the next wave of change hits their current organisation, I bet they will be among the first to be let go.

I understand that the idea of consciously adopting an experimental mindset feels risky for many of us. Thanks to our ridiculously static education and societal systems that take pride in preparing us to fit and feed the 'this is how things are culture', self-exploration and trying out are not our everyday cup of tea.

I encourage you to take some time off to reflect on your life journey so far. What are the moments that have prevented you from naturally exploring your interests, passions and talents? Once you put the finger on the underlying causes for your limited or lack of experimentation mindset, begin to address those. Only by doing so will you be able to take the ideas in this chapter forward.

Another essential mindset worth keeping in mind is that as you embark on your career experiments, one thing is certain: your outcomes will vary.

Assume that your experiments lead you to an unexpected career destination. This is perfectly OK as you are conscious of the circumstances that you got here. You are confident that you can make the most of the opportunities at hand; after all, your potential is limitless, right?

Furthermore, suppose you end up right back where you started after all your hard work. You will welcome yourself back joyfully. Self-assured that this is the best path for you at the moment.

In addition, it's unlikely not to encounter pit stops and detours in your experiments that will tempt you to feel defeated. In these moments, take time to zoom out and inquire, "What could be the luck-dawn hidden in this event that looks like a failure?" "What else am I not seeing?", "What can I learn and take with me moving forward?"

If playing around with your career still sounds scary, consider this. When scientists conduct experiments, they primarily focus on gaining new knowledge. With every new level of awareness, they make a conscious decision on the best next move. Sometimes it's 10-15 years of trial and error, patiently waiting to hit the jackpot.

I bet several deadly events manifest over such long periods; something bursts, someone loses a finger, someone pushes over the table with the specimens, and it's back to the drawing board. A guinea pig develops new symptoms, and no one can explain what is going on for months; the brightest guy in the room wakes up one day and says, "I am out of here," and so on.

What do the rest of the scientists and researchers do? They rise the next day, straighten their coats and get back to work. After all, the entire world is watching them and waiting patiently (not!) for them to deliver hope. Even if that hope is dressed as a vague statement like, "We are making progress, there seems to be light at the end of the tunnel". Which basically means nothing and everything at the same time, so we hold onto it.

This is what experiments do for us. They give us a ray of light strong enough to keep us interested and engaged in pursuing our growth in an uncertain world of work.

The four hats you have to wear in your career experiments

In every human soul are millions of ideas and desires that silently scream for attention. Sadly, many of these will never come to life because our fears silence them, or we fail to find small, creative ways of testing them to find out whether they are worth our attention.

This is where career experiments come in. They help you move rapidly through your endless list of career interests or curiosities, filtering and discarding everything that doesn't propel you forward.

Let's define a career experiment as the intentional art and science of pursuing an inquiry about your aspirations to gather valuable insights that will guide your career decisions.

First, let's explore a few foundational ideas. Experiments can be messy, and they can be magical. They can be loads of fun, and they can sometimes drain the life out of you. There is also no single path or right way of carrying out experiments. Once you set your intentions, go on and play in the best way possible. While at it, garner as many lessons. Relax into the process and let the journey unfold as it is. Treat every outcome as an information-gathering opportunity about your strengths, interests and skills.

To succeed in your experiments, embody the spirit of these four hats: the artist, the free, the scientist, the inventor and the free child-like wonder. Wearing each hat at the right time makes your experience more wonder-full and more insight-full.

As the artist, allow your imagination to go wild, dream of many possibilities, and develop the courage to follow your intuition. To create a new path for yourself, you will need to experiment with your talents and interests, often starting with a blank canvas. Thus, adopting the spirit of creating where nothing exists and the bravery and boldness to stand up for your worth when no one else believes in you is part of your journey. Yes, often, you will be doubtful. And this is great. These moments are a gift to build your self-belief. As an artist, you will need to know and embody your unique approach and talents. And to overcome the fears that hold you back from expressing yourself as your most natural and best self.

The scientist. Because pursuing your specific career experiments will require a systematic, focused approach. Trying out your interests and talents in small and different ways, documenting your findings, analysing your learning, and iterating until you find what works for you. Whether it's figuring out the right type of work for you or the ideal workplace that allows you to thrive, this approach is a gem. The scientist reminds you that just because you are trying out different things doesn't mean you approach and move through them haphazardly.

There is a way to play intentionally and still have lots of fun. We will explore more on this soon!

Designing and evolving your career in an unpredictable world also demands you sometimes wear the **inventor's hat.** To be an inventor is to be passionately driven by goals bigger than yourself. To maintain a high level of curiosity and inquisitive nature as you conduct your career experiments because you know the magical moment will happen unexpectedly. You are not afraid to take risks, and you continue to accelerate your growth, so you stay ahead of the game. Your experiments are designed to pursue uncharted waters and to position yourself as a forward-thinking, trendsetting professional in your field. You approach your career with an unyielding belief and patience in yourself and the journey you are on.

The free child-like wonder hat invites you to forget everything you think you know about yourself. To drop all the limitations you've put on what is possible for you and your capabilities.

Wearing this hat means you allow yourself to reignite the excitement you once had about your talents and dreams. You step into the unknown, unafraid of falling. You have complete trust that you can always find a way out of anything and everything. You commit to fully embracing that playful, lively and spontaneous spirit and to joyfully adopting new learning along your career journey. And finally, you are in touch with your innate wonders and magic that you may have forgotten somewhere along the way of 'life happening'. Your professional life takes up a significant percentage of your everyday life. Imagine how fulfilling life would be if you lived through your career adventures with a little more humour, lightheartedness, and play?

Finally, it was through experimentation that we progressed from cave dwellers eating raw meat to smoking it. OK, maybe there hasn't been much progress there, but yeah, it's how we discovered fire. Everything surrounding you wouldn't be in existence if no one took the chance to play around with stuff. Their patience and persistence to see what would emerge if they stretched their playfulness a little further resulted in great inventions. Intentionally or by accident, they noticed new events unfold, maintained their curiosity, played some more, noted the patterns, drew learnings, made changes small or big, perhaps sometimes causing dangerous eruptions and voilá another human problem was solved. This is the journey of every human who embarks on reinventing any aspect of their life. And your career advancement or transition journey is no exception.

In summary, to make the most of your experiments, master the ability to wear and juggle different hats, all at the same time. Tap your imagination to broaden your possibilities, follow a systematic approach and draw concrete insights. Stay spontaneous and playful so that you are open to spot and receive emerging opportunities. And finally, keep reinventing yourself so you can stay relevant and competitive in your field.

Your hats in action

Which of the four hats do you need to integrate more into how you navigate your career journey?

How would wearing each of these hats help you move ahead more calmly and confidently?

In what small ways can you start to embody the ways of the artist, the scientist, the free child-like wonder and the inventor in your everyday actions and behaviours?

How might your career experiments look like?

Experiments are only impactful when we approach them intentionally. Before you kick off trying out different interests, remember your purpose is to explore alternative opportunities that could need your talents, skills and strengths, now or in the future. In addition, aim to keep your experiments exciting with a considerable level of challenge, practicability and safety.

Suppose you have recently lost your job or desperately seek to shift from one profession, industry or workplace to another. Maybe you are hungry for a complete career overhaul. How and where do you get started?

How about trying out upcoming opportunities in promising & futuristic industries like artificial intelligence and biotechnology? Sounds scary? Not that easy to jump into? OK, then what about going back to something you picked up briefly and abandoned years ago? Or revisit roles you've had a secret crush on for decades and haven't gotten to do much about it? What was that thing your former colleagues used to say you were good really at, but you brushed their compliments and your attention to it aside? You probably have two or three of such. How about starting there? Right now?

Commit to three hours a week. Perhaps you will devote your time and skills to assisting a local startup or non-profit that is pursuing a mission that is close to your interests and passions. Do you know there are several websites where you can offer your expertise pro-bono globally? Consider devoting six or ten months to sharpening dormant skills and talents while broadening your market intelligence in the space you want to enter. This, without a doubt, broadens your perspective on what is possible for you.

Even if you are an expert in the field you wish to support, you are likely to know or be skilled at something that is currently lacking in those organisations. Besides, you can always learn! Your input will undoubtedly add incremental value to their work, give you new knowledge, and strengthen your experimentation muscles.

Additionally, you could choose to spend a few extra hours a week in a different department in your current organisation. Assuming your management is not made up of dream killers. Choose activities that allow you to gain valuable exposure and insights and the opportunity for you to contribute without disrupting the team's energy and attention too much.

While at it, stay present. Remember the Wu Wei concept discussed earlier? (chapter 2) Yeah, that. Stay aware so that you can capture how your career experiments are unfolding. You don't want to go through your trials blindly.

With time and consistency, you will soon notice a significant transformation in how you view your current state, the value of your strengths and give you a taste of whether the move you have in mind is what you truly want.

Take note and often reflect on how your experiences are evolving:

What do you like about the tasks or activities you are trying out?

Be real. How do you honestly feel when taking part in this type of work? Does the idea of spending the rest of your life pursuing similar work excite you?

What new insights and questions have emerged now that you're living your dream?

What can you conclude after a few weeks, let's say six, of engaging in this type of work?

Oh, and remember, no, you don't need to take yourself so seriously (chapter 1). Afterall, you are just playing. You know that experiments are stepping stones to your higher goals, so you don't move in a rush. You are calm. Furthermore, avoid emotional attachments or taking your findings from your trials as conclusions. Like a scientist, you are merely seeking additional knowledge that will help you carve out a smarter path to your destination. Be patient then, because…

You will fail anyway. Oh no, I meant, you will meet your luck-dawns

Many of them, as a matter of fact.

You know you can try something and be great at it. While in other cases, it might turn out you suck at certain roles or tasks big time. For me, experimenting with complex computation tasks or engaging my brain in highly structured and detailed work has proven to be a source of misery over time. I have also made peace with it.

Years back, I gave a shot to pursuing a typical career path; getting into a stable organisation with a steady job, slowly climbing the ladder, and making it to management in 5 or 6 years. Initially, I thought I was committed to this path. But who was I kidding, faking patience? Not my thing. Rocket speed is more of my soul's calling. I had already led global teams exceptionally well in my previous roles. Why did I have to wait so long to advance to a position of strategic leadership? Of course, I realised all this in retrospect years later.

After nine months in a stable and secure job world, I remembered one of my fantasies, to work for a multinational company.

Immediately I chased this moment of intuition, searched, and landed a management role leading a global career acceleration program in Mumbai.

To the world around me, I had failed at following the standard path to success. Was this risky giant leap of faith scary? Hell yes! What if I hated living in this new country? What if my new job sucked? What if I failed at leading a global team? What if I didn't gel with the new team? What if I didn't get another stable job when I got back? What if bla bla bla. Yup, I had all these monkeys haunting me all the way to the airport boarding gate until I remembered …

The Safety Paradox

'I don't have a choice'. These words can be terrifying. When they enter your career vocabulary, it's a sign you've hit a dead-end. The options for what is possible for you are now limited by your preconceived notions.

Humans love to have choices as they give us two benefits; a sense of freedom and a sense of safety. If this doesn't work out, I can try plans b, c or z. We will do anything possible to avoid feeling out of choice.

With today's fast-changing world of work and our reptilian brain still heavily invested in running our inner world, our need for safety has heightened. Most people find uncertainty to be unsettling. Strange as it may sound, as risky and scary as it is, experimentation or playing with the unfamiliar is our safest bet for building a pool of quality options in our careers.

We are caught in a strange place. To create the sense of safety we need, we must take on the habit of trying out new career challenges, ideas or opportunities that may sometimes petrify us.

How do we navigate this paradox?

The best way to prepare for the unknown is to anticipate it and take action today to cushion us when the future arrives. Hence, trying things that call on our spirit is not an option. Once an individual narrows down the activities that engage their attention the most, the next step is to build depth and expertise in these areas purposefully.

Recognise that, at least in the beginning, there is no formula for experimentation. You will need to move past your worries about where to start and simply start. Take action in any direction of your choice. Soon, as you observe the emerging patterns and begin to connect your own dots, you will realise that you are creating your own formula along the way. And that is why you will succeed. You will have found a way that uniquely works for you.

The more action one takes out of their safety zone, the more their capabilities will surprise them, the more their confidence grows and the more their sense of safety rises. One moment you are thinking, "I never knew I could do that, and now I do! I wonder what else I can experiment with". Why? Your world of possibilities is opening up, offering you supplementary choices, despite the erratic changes in your industry or profession.

So go ahead. Experiment with the idea that you've been holding back for so long, as it feels edgy. Have you been contemplating taking a part-time role outside your normal scope of work? Or have you been playing with the idea of monetising your hobby? Do it. Hesitation steals time, talent, and opportunities.

You will run out of fuel, so bring some madness along

Experiments take time and require you to engage your mental and physical energy fully. Some trials will backfire. In other seasons, the temptation to hang out in your zone of safety will be stronger than your will to try out your ideas. These moments require you to be gentle with yourself. And to unleash some dose of madness that will keep your fire burning.

When I run out of fuel, and so will you countless times, first, I pause. Nothing beats a long deep breath and a 2-minute gaze into nothingness.

I then try to picture the great marathoners in history, taking pride in those from my region, East Africa. Running through the vast, hostile terrain, the harsh winds and, some days, completely worn out, yet never taking their focus from their end game. To one day set a record of who they are—the greatest runners in the world. We will never know the truth about the numerous trials they endured to set a world record. But one thing is certain. They must be firm believers in their power and potential. On other days, I dream of the Pharaohs. You must see the tallest pyramid, Khufu, built about 4,500 years ago. Or read about the explorer Vasco Da Gama-four ships, 170 men, one mission, to be the first Europeans to reach India by sea. Through storms, scurvy, sharks, and all, they made it to Malindi, Kenya, then to Mumbai, India.

"How much faith did these humans have in themselves and their abilities?" I ponder. It must have been a lot. Faith in yourself, do you have that?

Such individuals, I think, must have been mad humans. Driven by a strong desire and commitment to adventure, they become unstoppable in the pursuit of the impossible. They bet on themselves and went all the way. Among other factors, faith in self, courage, and a dose of madness must have kept them taking those tiny bravely into the unknown and eventually propelling them to succeed.

How mad are you about your career aspirations? About all those gifts and possibilities that lie inside you?

If you truly believed in yourself, would you stick around playing poker with your infinite potential?

Would you fancy embodying even a fraction of the spirit of the mad humans in history who made the impossible eventually possible through tiny little steps?

Eight mindsets for running transformative learning-oriented career experiments

You must have crossed paths with people who were pursuing various ideas and interests, but none of them developed into anything concrete. There is no phenomenal reason behind this disaster. They simply failed at the onset to lay out a clear purpose and measures of success for their trials.

You can not afford to go frantically into your experiments. Intend to keep the scientist's hat on all the time. Treat your trials as discovery opportunities. Plan for reflection moments. Take this time to evaluate your learning and integrate the insights into your subsequent career decisions and actions. If the latter is not happening, you are wasting your time.

Here are eight vital mindsets you need to embody to ensure your experiments are intentional, learning-focused and have an end-game in mind.

Don't overthink where to start

You could experiment with one of the many secret dreams and talents you would love to see come alive. Those desires you hardly mention to anyone. Maybe you feel afraid people will think you are crazy? When did sane humans ever achieve anything great?

You may be thinking at this moment, "I get all this, Martha, but I need clarity on what to experiment with. I have so many ideas", or "I am so clueless about where to start".

Pay little attention to overthinking what the first experiment should be or when it is appropriate to begin. The clarity you are seeking can only be gained through action and then refined for a lifetime. So, get moving.

You can choose to take a paper and pen right now and note down three random alternative ways you could start spending your time, talents and energy, and possibly be paid for it. Then commit a few hours over the next few weeks to deeply experimenting with each.

To become a master of experimentation, keep reading.

Begin with a clear learning intention

With every experiment, you must be on to something. Before taking action, set a clear learning intention that illustrates what you are curious to test and gain new knowledge of. These are the objectives that help you keep track of how your experiments are unfolding.

Primarily, every intention should lead you to higher levels of self-awareness and clarity about the type of work that allows you to create value naturally.

To keep the curious mind switched on, define your intentions in a question format.

An exciting and challenging intention sets the pace for your adventure. So, keep an explorative and enthusiastic spirit.

You are probably bored with the way things are in your career anyway. Besides, some playfulness and lightness will keep you going when the mud gets thick.

Below are a few examples of learning intentions from my past career adventures. You will find the background stories for each at the end of this chapter.

"What type of corporate environment would allow me to thrive?"

"How might I feel if I was working in a highly structured global organisation with over 400,000 people?"

"How would I fit into a role as a global recruiter?"

"How could my skills and abilities add value in a fast-changing business?"

"What would it feel like if I was working in education innovation, changing the game of how children learn?" "What would an ideal role in the human resources field potentially look like for me?"

Let your first list be limitless. Once you have concluded, don't fret; pick any three that make your heart jump the most when you think of immersing in them and get moving. Remember to stay awake while at it, so those opportunities in disguise don't escape you. You never want to miss a luck-dawn moment.

To sprint or marathon?

The nature of your learning intentions, your current career realities and, of course, your fitness level, determine the time you allocate and the pace at which you move to accomplish your mission.

Can you be an apprentice and master two different skill sets in a year? Can you monetise two hobbies in the same year? On top of your 60 hour work week, can you manage to run three pro-bono consulting gigs in 6 months? Or should you just take one that runs for an extended period?

Maybe, maybe not. Figure out and make peace with what is manageable within your context and commit to that.

Set an end date

Never begin without an end date in mind. Having a set date helps you navigate a couple of potential pitfalls.

Keeping your experiments open-ended will trap you in a state of endless testing. "I'm still figuring it out," is a common phrase on the streets of little progression. Keep off.

Experiments that are done well can be playful, fun and addictive. Stay alert to recognise when you are in it just for the thrill.

Discipline yourself to set reasonable dates that give you the rush to get to the end while you remain somewhat grounded. Balance is the key.

Some experiments can be completed in a few weeks, while others will take you several months. I leave it to you to determine your timeline. Of course, you can adjust these as needed; let them not be, though, because you took no action.

Keep a record of your observations

Once your cameras are rolling, and you are entirely in action mode, you are ready to learn! Create a system that allows you to capture your observations and insights in real-time. This helps you keep their essence alive.

You will notice how you feel about specific roles, industries, certain tasks, work environments, projects, colleagues, etc. Record the intriguing realisations about yourself as you continue to immerse yourself in different worlds. What feels exhilarating? What sucked the energy out of you? What was challenging but surprisingly energising? Set a time to zoom in and out of these observations. In this time, connect the dots, spot hidden opportunities and map out paths for integration.

Slay your way through the action

Develop a laser-like focus on action. Allow nothing to divert your attention, as a monk would.

Get rid of all obstructions and invest your time and efforts in getting through your most important experiments. Impeccably well. Once they are complete, you will not be the same person. Neither will your career trajectory.

Follow the curiosity within the curiosity

With every move, surprises will emerge, unexpected clues, and new insights that leave you even more curious. Depending on what you are learning and other external factors outside your control, you might need to take a detour or an extended pitstop. Like we all did during the global pandemic in 2020. Many of us had to seek other means of livelihood (detour) or simply wait for the storm to pass (pitstop).

At first, these may appear as distractions. Be slow in dismissing them. Hang out with them, flip them over, sit with them in the dark, burn incense if you must, talk them through with your confidants. "What are you here to teach me?" is a common question at these times. Keep your heart open, so you are ready to receive the answers when they are revealed.

Military-style review

Be ruthless in reviewing your progress.

How do you honestly feel about how your career experiments are unfolding? What are you learning about your strengths and opportunities for growth? What kind of work do you realise you'll struggle with? Pursuing such would be a waste of your time and talents. What has held you back in the past from fully carrying out your experiments? How do you feel when you immerse yourself in your areas of interest? What support would help you move ahead faster with your experiments?

Find no reason to justify your lack of action. Fire up your inner warrior and stay committed to your learning path. Review your learning and tweak your approaches quickly during your Sacred Career Spaces.

Stories from my own career experiments

Wondering how all this career experimentation stuff pans out practically? Grab some popcorn.

My bachelor's degree was in Early Childhood Education. In summary, we spent several hours diving into human psychology, child development, the role of parenting and social interactions in character development, aka, how this screws us up, how kids learn, and effective ways of structuring learning experiences for 2 to 9-year-olds.

Back then, if anyone told me I would forever be grateful for my university degree, I would have easily dismissed them.

Yet, they would have been right. This degree opened a whole world for me. Learning at an early age how human brains work, how personalities are shaped, and how childhood upbringing and trauma shape our adult lives raised my awareness of being a better human for future generations and made me conscious of how these early experiences also shape our professional lives.

What many people don't know is that I landed on this path, not by choice. Long story short, my uncle, tired of the endless & frustrating university application processes, took a deep sigh and said, "Go study education, because as a teacher, you will never lack a job". He is a wise man.

And just like that, my future was sealed. As an A student, becoming a teacher was the last career path I was expected to follow. Thus, that signature felt like my sentence to doom. All my life, I have been groomed to believe my path was in medicine, law, engineering or other scientific fields. Sounds familiar?

Now, I am sure you are wondering where the experiments come in, so here we go.

1st experiment

While at university, I worked as a radio show host for our university radio station. I know it has nothing to do with early childhood education. To be honest, I spent more time participating in extracurricular activities than I did on schoolwork, and yet I graduated with honors. I was an intentional and dedicated experimenter with my interests and passions. Back then, journalism was one of my interests.

I was also curious about creating remarkable experiences. This is why I spent three consecutive years volunteering as a key organiser of the university's annual career fair as well. In addition, I also worked as a student leader in a global leadership program.

Though I was partly escaping from the boredom of formal education, I was sowing the seeds of career experimentation in retrospect.

Communicating ideas, mentoring and creating inspiring learning spaces have always been my areas of interest, even before I went to university. The activities on campus gifted me the golden opportunity to see my interests in action.

Furthermore, I needed a backup plan *(choices)*. Back then, the career paths for my bachelor's were unclear. Instead of panicking or changing to 'high potential' courses (keeping in mind unemployability was already big back then), I chose a different approach. To maximise my talents and acquire additional competitive skills beyond classwork. By my graduation date, I had acquired a pocket full of diverse experiences and skill sets that opened up a wide range of potential professional paths.

All these seemingly unrelated experiences were geared towards my learning intention. "How might I develop my talents and interests in unorthodox ways, thus increasing my professional options four years down the line?"

Did it work? Like magic, as you will see in the following experiments.

2nd experiment

Straight out of university, I briefly worked as a tutor for early childhood educators. When I accepted the teaching job offer, my learning mission was clear. *"How might a role in preparing diploma level students to be early childhood educators enable me to make the best use of my talents, gifts, energy, and time?"*

I resigned four months later.

The quitting process was birthed when I realised I would never enrol my children in schools where the teachers I trained taught. I detested the lifeless approach to learning I had been hired to uphold. While my sweet spot is co-creating with learners in the design of engaging, challenging and transformative learning experiences, here I was expected to transfer information that anyone could read from their textbooks.

Initially, I convinced myself that I had to stay. I hung onto a false enthusiasm that encouraged me to keep going. Until I couldn't anymore.

So I quit my first job after university. It was risky but not riskier than settling down so early in my career in a role that would use none of my abilities and talents.

The third experiment

As I contemplated leaving my tutoring job, I spent several moments reflecting on, "What else am I good at?" "Working with people," I remembered. This was one of the most consistent pieces of feedback I received during my university volunteering experiences. Then I asked myself, "What can I do with that?" What are the different career options for people who excel at working with others?

With my limited knowledge and not much external guidance, I came up with the only familiar answer, "Human Resources".

The only issue was that I had no prior experience in human resources. Being sceptical if any company would give me a chance, I posed a new question to myself: "What alternative experiences have work activities that mirror this field and thus would give me the space to utilise my talents while building a foundation for transferrable HR skills?"

Fast forward, I headed to Tanzania for a talent management role for a young professionals employability & upskilling leadership program. Here, I advanced my HR skills by taking on functions such as creating a strong organisational brand, supervising member engagement activities, managing new member recruitment, and designing learning and development journeys.

This experience gave me a feel of the world of human resources from a distance. As I closely observed my performance and connection with the different tasks, I kept evaluating: "What would an ideal role in the human resources field potentially look like for me?"

In the process, through a lot of self-driven learning, I fast-tracked my skillset in enormous ways that no entry-level job would have exposed me to. These included; designing learning experiences, conference management, facilitation and training, organisation development, team management, and partnership building. A decade-plus later, many of these remain highly relevant in my everyday job.

As this role came to an end, I thought I was ready to 'settle down'. This turned out to be a big fat lie to myself. I failed again. Which brings us to...

A series of several other experiments

When I got back to Kenya, I secured a job at an innovative education institution. I went into this role hoping to learn, "What would it feel like if I was working as an education innovator, changing how children learn?

This role marked my shortest ever experiment. After three weeks, I had to leave. For three reasons. 1) I had achieved my monthly deliverables in one week, and it was unclear how I would spend the rest of the month. 2) I received another offer for a role in recruiting that I had applied for earlier. And 3) I still had a couple of experiments I was committed to trying out. The recruitment role seemed like a better use of my talents, time, energy, and an entry point into what 'real' corporate looks and feels like for human resources professionals. I figured this was my luck-dawn to make a move.

Was this risky, terrifying and somewhat rushed from an external perspective? Yes, yes, yes! Without a mentor or guide to seek counsel from, taking this decision brought turmoil. I mean, who quits their job after three weeks, right? Partly, my intuition gave me the courage to jump. Looking back, I am happy I made the move; otherwise, that would have been a perfect opportunity to get stuck. The warning signs were crystal clear from day one. This would not be an organisation that would allow my talents to thrive. It was riskier not to dive into corporate HR finally.

Since then, I've met many people who feel stuck in the same job for ten or even fifteen years. It's fascinating to have them reflect and point to the exact moment when they missed the window of opportunity to leave. As a result, they accumulate too many years in workspaces and roles that don't serve their potential.

Other times, I have encountered professionals who leave 'great roles' within the first six months. Why? They have mastered how to identify the traps that will hinder their growth early enough. They put in work defining the workplace that will allow them to fully utilise their skills and express their unique abilities in creating value. I'm not advocating for people to quit their jobs, but I am advocating for greater efficiency in how we spend our time, energy, and talents. This is a less painful path for both employers and professionals.

This role in India was the culmination of all my years of career experiments. It was also the stepping stone that launched my entrepreneurial adventures and my current career chapter as a trusted advisor for fast-growing organisations in emerging markets and career coaching. Having spent several hours reflecting on how I wanted to experience my next role and how success would feel, my ideal path for maximum value creation was clear.

The ability to create, lead and be a catalyst for accelerating the growth of innovative social and economic solutions and unleashing the potential of individuals in emerging markets. The more I invest my time, energy, and talents in work that allows me to come up with big, impactful ideas, rally people behind them, and help them get off the ground quickly, the more value I create and the more fulfilling my work becomes.

Chapter 7

TRANSITION IS NOT AN OVERNIGHT ADVENTURE

Career transitioning?

How you probably see it...

A process that has a start and end date.

A destination you can't wait to arrive at. A 'new' or 'better job.

Your transferable skills are adequate for your cross over.

What you need to pay more attention to...

Being strategic & intentional. Embracing an enduring spirit. Gently holding space for yourself. Cultivating mastery of your limiting thoughts. Embodying an undying enthusiasm.

These super mindsets are your secret weapons for a successful career transition.

Go go gently

"Today I escaped anxiety. Or no, I discarded it, because it was within me, in my own perceptions — not outside." — Marcus Aurelius.

If you've ever traversed rural Nepal, specifically taking the infamous treacherous route from Tatopani (the home of the hot water springs in the Annapurna region) to Pokhara by a local bus, then you agree with me; it's one hell of a ride!

Your fear of the unknown strikes at the sight of the inscription on the local buses at the Tatopani station - "Fear Nothing", they remind you. You may have escaped heavy snowfalls, avalanches and acute mountain sickness, perhaps 4000-5000 meters high, yet these words somehow manage to inflict an uncomfortable level of trepidation in you.

Then there are your drivers who portray a state indescribable. While the locals mesmerise you with their sharp and focused look that is so serious yet so zen. Once the conductors pack a few tonnes on the roof of the bus, including a couple of goats and beds, you are ready to depart.

A few meters out of the bus station, you realise the road is un tarmacked. You will be driving on the edge of a cliff on a rough and bumpy road for over eight hours. You are lucky if you don't lose your teeth from being thrown up and down. Your journey might take fourteen hours because, well, you had to make several stops to make way for the falling rocks.

On the contrary, the route is stunning! Breathtaking mountains, sparkling rivers all along, and tiny little villages keep popping up. The sky is graciously clear on a good day, and the soft warm sun solidifies your beautiful memories.

The journey takes all your daylight hours. You could be shitting your pants all through, cursing the dreadful road and the system that refuses to fix it. Or, you could model the zen state of the locals who have taken this same road all their lives. You could choose to enjoy the endless magnificent nature along the way, trusting you will arrive in one piece, or you could hold your breath all the way to Pokhara.

You choose.

As I sat through this journey, partly terrified, partly amazed, I couldn't help but ponder over how significantly our attention impacts our experience. Focus on the harshness, and thus your life becomes. Focus on gentleness, and so is your reality. Two humans could be travelling on this same route yet experience very different journeys.

This couldn't be more true than in our career journeys. The terrain can be cold, unfamiliar, and sometimes rough. Some roads may end abruptly. Others may be impassable, forcing us to divert or turn back. It can also be dramatically delightful, shockingly grand, and fulfilling. How we meet and indulge in these events highly impacts how we feel and experience the different phases of our careers.

As we transition through different phases of our career journeys, a few events are inevitable. We will get tossed in all directions. We will be cornered in situations beyond our control. The outcomes we desire will often be in another's hands. Changes will visit us faster than we can blink. Sometimes, we will be ill-prepared to meet these events. Our ability to gently hold space for ourselves as we patiently wait for our aspirations will be challenged.

Truthfully, travelling this way is exhausting. How might we navigate our journeys more smoothly? More compassionately?

The challenge posed to us is acceptance. Total surrender to the fact that our progress, decisions, and critical milestones in our careers lie in the hands of multiple stakeholders.

Every event that unfolds contrary to our expectations is an invitation—an invitation to be gentle on our minds. Seek to understand rather than criticise ourselves for the misfortunes that befall us. Remember, we have the power within to untangle ourselves from whatever our professions throw our way. When our growth curve moves at a snail pace or when every call bears only obstacles to our dreams, patience is the answer. An invitation to realise that with every misadventure lies hidden treasures that are our stepping stones.

This is a tough call that provokes us to shift our thinking and perceptions of self, the world of work, our employers, workplaces, and so on. Human as we are, we would rather not. Hence instead of looking within and allowing the mysteries of our experience to guide our way, we are quick to take control and turn events around. We react swiftly. As a result, we fall for unuseful and hasty solutions, like settling for the first tempting and lesser evil opportunity that we come across. Before we know it, we find ourselves in the same rat hole we briefly escaped. We are lucky, if not worse. Our impatience and lack of strategic and intentional reflection and action trap us in cycles of stuckness.

This is probably a good moment for you to pause and enquire within. In what bumpy areas in your career are you criticising yourself too much? How might you allow more gentleness and compassion to yourself?

As an alpha female, gentleness and self-compassion have been a myth for most of my life. Hence it is ironic that I choose to address these. However, my passion for advocating for these as crucial ingredients in our career advancement adventures goes beyond my troubles. As a recruiter and management consultant for over a decade, I can confidently assure you many of the reasons you criticise yourself in your career, especially when things don't go your way, are untrue. And thus not worth what it costs your wellbeing.

Over the years, I have worn many hats in the recruitment field. As an advisor to hiring managers, a headhunter, interviewer, and competency assessor. These have shed a lot of light on all the juicy stuff that goes behind hiring decisions. Secrets that have nothing to do with the candidates but are solely meant to safeguard the organisation's wellbeing.

"We suffer more in imagination than in reality," says Seneca (the stoic philosopher from the 4-5th BC). Unfortunately, this is the reality for many of us. Trying to make sense of how and why our job applications ended without an offer letter, why that recruiter disappeared after your great conversation. Or why your colleague got promoted instead of you, leads to spikes in imagination and self-created incomplete truths. When set on replay, these take us straight to the valley of misery.

It saddens me to see professionals walk around heavily burdened. Oblivious that there are diverse odds and interests of players that must align for one's career desires to manifest, we indulge in setting unrealistic transition and advancement expectations and make assumptions about recruiting teams. Over time, these assumptions become our gospel truth, which we feed into our self-pity parties—eventually leading us to helplessness.

Before we know it, the self-destructive art of judging ourselves against our standards or those set by others emerges. And this judgement comes in many forms: Making conclusions about our character and our abilities, getting discouraged from comparing ourselves with others, downplaying our chances, determining the ceiling for our future achievements and so on.

We need to stop.

Maybe you are thinking: "Nah, I don't judge myself." Ok, I give you the benefit of doubt; however, do you find yourself judging others at times? For standards that you've set for yourself?

Judging others is a form of what psychology calls projection. I call it the *no-sense* in my head. Because when carefully evaluated, it really makes no sense. If you too assess carefully the no-sense in your head, you will realise it is nowhere close to reality. Neither is it a true reflection of who you are and what you are capable of.

When we project, we extend unto others what we are afraid to confront in ourselves. It's a smart way our brains found to survive. And it works every time in keeping us safe. We judge, we feel better. Even if it's temporary.

The more I reflect on how I judge others and their actions, the closer I get home to how I judge myself, especially in areas I haven't fully embraced.

Self-judgment is a detrimental habit that takes a real toll on our careers. Learning to take the observer's seat when the judgement of self or the other strikes, becoming aware of what we are projecting and holding ourselves gently is valuable in your journey.

All this judging works in autopilot mode in our subconscious. So at first, when you hear it, it sounds ridiculous. I, too, rebelled against this idea until I engaged myself with the judging game. A game I am inviting you to play.

It's pretty straightforward.

Next time you find your mind tempted to judge others' career choices, actions or behaviours, pause. Redirect this attention back to yourself and ask, "Wait, Martha (replace with your name), in what ways are you judging yourself at this moment?"

The no-sense in your head

Once you begin to focus your attention on the thousands of thoughts criss crossing your mind at every moment, first you will be shocked. Second, you will notice the nagging no-sense in your head often sounds like this:

I am not good enough to qualify for such an incredible role

I suck at this task big time!

I am terrible at interviewing

He is not as great as he thinks he is

I don't deserve to rise to that level this early in my career

She will never make it in such a field

It takes people decades to earn that amount of money; who am I kidding thinking I am worth it?

I need more time to learn before I jump into such roles

There is no way Joseph can succeed in such a role

That's probably the worst move they could have taken in their career

This is the best I can do

I will never be as great as Judy!

…

Any of these sound familiar?

This is mind boggling when you remember this fun fact. Did you know that your brain processes about 50-80,000 thoughts per day? Scientists are still figuring out the exact figure. In the meanwhile, do the Math to find out what this number translates to per second. And then, just to spice things up, consider this: 70-80% of all those thoughts are negative.

Boom!

Now imagine how this way of thinking could impact your career adventures?! Most of the time, you are obsessing over the harsh realities of your situation and overly focusing on the things going haywire. Constantly worrying; "What if I never get another job? What if I am stuck in this job forever? What if my industry never recovers?" Judging yourself after every interview. Comparing your career progress with others. Dismissing your achievements as not great enough. Worrying again, "What if my savings run out?" A good thought to have and plan for, but spending most of your time thinking about it takes your attention, energy, and time from creating what you want in the first place.

All this no-sense makes the idea of gentleness an impossible and elusive pursuit.

Luckily science has proven we can rewire how our brains respond to specific events and the meaning we give to our experiences—especially unpleasant ones. You may have heard of neuroplasticity? The ability of the brain to change and adapt as a result of new experiences? In our careers, we can achieve this by accelerating our exposure to new ways of thinking, taking up new tasks, pursuing new interests such as our long-abandoned hobbies, modelling new positive traits, learning new skills, engaging in enriching conversations and making new professional connections. Simply put, choose to shift your attention and energy to something more awe-inspiring than the misadventures of your career.

Novelty is queen in shifting how we experience our career journeys. That 'I am stuck feeling' arises when we get too used to the mundane ways of our work. Same problem solving approaches, same old colleagues, same lunch conversations often dominated by one person, same routes to work and all. If you are reading this, chances are you have a strong desire to experience the new often. Newness makes our lives interesting, keeps our brains young, alters our perspectives, and distracts our attention from the chaos. It's thus crucial for you to craft strategic and intentional opportunities along your career journey where you plug in and deeply immerse yourself in experiences out of your norm. This is not only good for your mental wellbeing but also helps clear any blocks that hinder you from seeing yourself and your career through new lenses.

Before you proceed, pause and commit to immersing yourself in at least one new and out of your way activity every single week! Observe keenly how this shifts the ideas and thoughts you have of yourself.

If you are immensely pumped to learn more about letting go of the no-sensical thoughts in your head, fast track yourself to chapter 7!

Ride on Enthusiasm

When have you ever achieved anything without a little spark of madness? Seriously, review your most phenomenal accomplishments so far and ask yourself this question.

Or look around and spot a couple of humans achieving epic stuff in their lives. Don't they sometimes confuse you with their happy foolness? It's actually happy fullness, but you probably don't see it that way *yet*. Even when their worlds get shaken up, don't they seem to possess a fire that never burns out?

Several times, I have been acknowledged for being highly energetic, enthusiastic, and full of life. "Where do you get all that energy from?", some people ask. The other day someone mentioned that when I step into a room, everything lights up. How can I not be? My goals alone activate volcanos. Interestingly, I have friends whose energy and enthusiasm for life make mine seem meagre. There is a spectrum to how we manifest our inner fire, but we all have nevertheless.

To fully tap and fan our inactive zeal, we must be driven by career goals bigger than our troubles. Our troubles keep us short-sighted. With big dreams and bold goals, we have little space in our heads for *no-sense.* Instead, we are powered up by a fierceness that elevates us above our misadventures. And we show up eager and forward-looking no matter what. *Do you have a goal that moves you this way?*

Let's say you've been seeking new opportunities. Not much is forthcoming. Now you feel stuck. What is the worst that could happen if you kept on going, jumping more hurdles with a smile on your face? What would you lose? You're probably allured by this idea right now. But you're also caught up by the no-sense whispering that it's too crazy to smile through your problems. Somewhere along the way, you picked the belief that problems must be met with a gloomy face, a broken smile, a heavy heart, and dragging feet. Your thinking is getting in the way. Journeying this way is not only tiresome but boring. If you are serious about creating significant shifts in your career, it's time to take a detour.

We cannot conclude without mentioning the impact of our relationships in our career journeys. Though we may be surrounded by dozens of humans in our professional life, we often feel alone in our journeys. Many of us have few to zero trusted confidants with whom we can genuinely share our career realities. Without such safe spaces to process and empty our troubles, it's easy to fall for scepticism and overwhelm when our professional lives are challenged. We cuddle by ourselves, paralysed not by lack of solutions but by overthinking the challenges we face. Consequently, we forget our innate playfulness and disregard our liveliness.

What if, right now, you got up and psyched yourself up about an idea, a secret desire, or an unspoken talent you are excited to pursue? Visualise yourself having achieved this in the near future. Allow yourself to feel the thrill of seeing this dream come to life move through your veins, now.

Or how about you put on your favourite music and dance around like a fool, pick up the phone, and call some other lucky, happy fool in your circle to join your party. I hear parties of two are a blast! Laugh at how ridiculous life has been lately. What the heck are the gods thinking? Go for a long wandering walk in the park. Play with your kids - this time for the sheer joy of it. Reminisce the long-gone days when the magic of youth and freedom filled your every breath. And all this career stuff was but a distant mirage. Soak in this wonderful energy and bring it back with you for the rest of your day. Do whatever "doing you" means to get past the no-sense in your head, so you can light up your spark of enthusiasm.

On some days, I dance for several minutes before starting a big, seemingly impossible project. It helps reboot my system to groundness. Several of my clients began integrating dancing into their interview preparation activities. It helps them get out their heads, relax and reconnect with their sense of wonder.

I have found that tricking my brain with positive language is a powerful way of reminding myself what I momentarily forget. I am the master of my mind. Never the other way round. So I scream my heart out, "I am extraordinary", "I got this!", "I am capable of more than I think I am".

I can count the hundreds of times this sort of silly sauciness has saved me from self-sabotage.

Headless chicken transitions

I have had hundreds of career conversations unfold like this.

Human: I need help navigating my career transition. I am hoping to move into a new industry.

Me: Sounds great! I am happy for you! I am curious, what inspired you to want to make this shift?

Human: You know... I want to grow... I want to progress... I want change... I want career growth (all those vague statements from the career copy-paste street).

Me: Ok, and in your transition journey so far, what action have you already taken?

Human: I have been applying for jobs in different industries. Nothing is coming through. I guess I don't get shortlisted because of my resume.

Me: Hmmm, tell me more.

Human: I think since my resume doesn't have relevant experience in the industry.

Me: And what else?

Human: I think the salary expectations I quote when I get a chance to interview are higher than the market rate.

Me: As you share all this, what are you realising?

In other words, what I like to call blind transitions.

Drawing from the above, a few traps to avoid:

- Lack of a compelling reason to transition (if you can't convince yourself in the mirror, how will you convince your future employer?).
- Assumptions of what could be the problem. For example your resume (though it could be the problem, most of the time, it's just the tip of the iceberg).
- Unaligned expectations, thinking that merely sending applications will magically communicate your transition intentions and grab the attention you deserve.

When I encounter such conversations with experienced professionals in high-level strategy roles, which also happens a lot, I often ask,

"Doesn't the same strategic approach you use in your work apply to your career?"

After a few seconds, I may receive a response like this, "Oh yeah, you may be right. I don't know why I never looked at the transition journey this way. I guess I have been approaching this all wrong. I must first get clear on what I want, why I want it, and what I am willing to sacrifice to get it. It seems I also need a more diverse and broad approach in connecting with professionals in the industry I want to move to. This will help me tap into a wider pool of opportunities. Perhaps I could also consider volunteering some of my free time in this new industry. This way I can learn a thing or two about the sector before committing to jump".

I am in constant awe at how professionals imagine career transitions as plug-and-play affairs—repeatedly ignoring all the prerequisites required to set themselves up for success. *A strategic transition journey will easily take you two years.* Starting with the idea's inception, to phases of deep reflection to uncover the layers of what you want and crafting a compelling story of why you want it. Thereafter, you still need to take up new opportunities, sometimes pro bono, to immerse yourself in your anticipated world of work. This is a great way to ascertain this is what you want. In the process, you get to identify potential risks and figure out how you may mitigate them. You also become aware of the areas you need to level up your expertise. Not to mention the several months or sometimes years in search it might take you to land on the perfect opportunity.

Encounters with unintentional career transition seekers take me back to my childhood. Growing up in the village, the ability to slaughter a chicken was a necessary life skill. Before heading to work, our parents would leave us instructions on which chicken was to be slaughtered by the time they got back home. Somehow I mastered the skill early enough; it's the beheading that often scared the shit out of me.

Once, I cut off the poor chicken's head, and the body ran away to the bushes. I was terrified because I knew that if I didn't trace the chicken, I would be the dinner. So I ran into the bushes, chasing the body. Even more terrified of bumping into other animals in the bushes. But I ran nevertheless. Dinner was served. Mom never found out (till now, lol). Childhood was fun.

Today, stepping back into that timeline, I often wonder, "Where the heck did this chicken think it was going? Did it really believe it would end up anywhere without its thinking body part?"

Here is a brief reflective exercise for you if you want to transition and advance your career more intentionally.

Do you know the 3-4 possible paths you could transition into? Oh, you don't? Start with a list of 10 ideas you could experiment with **(and kick off your experiments).** Or engage a career coach to dig into your experiences and help you draw and repackage your valuable and transferable skills.

Can you articulately and compellingly tell why each of these paths is best suited for you? Depending on your answer, you know what to do :)

What must die (not literally like the chicken, more like beliefs, behaviours, the no-sense in your head stuff) for you to get what you really want in your career? As you let go, expect the things that need to die to shoot little arrows of pain at you along the way. Take these as signs you're on the right path.

There never will be a perfect job. Hence once you've determined what you are seeking, map out the gains and pains of each possible path. And then get clear on what pains you are willing to endure. Without clarity on what you are ready to suffer for and what you must let go of, you will be stuck in inaction.

Finally, transition, advancing or revamping your career demands both your attention and effort. On a scale of 0-10, how ready do you feel you are to invest the effort and time needed to get to the next level? This is key! You want to make sure you are not just in love with the idea of getting to the other side but detest the work needed to get there.

Chapter 8

BECOMING THE MAGICIAN OF YOUR THOUGHTS

Gracious words are a honeycomb, sweet to the soul and healing to the bones. **Proverbs 16:24**

Our language is a reflection of our inner world. With every word, we reinforce our external experiences. Knowing our language carries potent forces, is the way you speak about your career encounters creating magic, relieving your burdens or piling up toxic energy that weighs you down? Are your adjectives a reflection of your best self? Do they fuel your dreams?

With the customary word abracadabra (Hebrew for I will create as I speak), a magician alters our reality.

What can we learn from this mystical profession?

A random Mumbai magician

Before I get started, I want to emphasise that this is a true story. I am not obliged to, but the whole unfolding was so bizarre that years later, I still don't believe it happened. I also don't recall why I was in a shared tuk-tuk in Mumbai. Or where I was headed.

I do remember, though, that it was one of those days I needed a good cheer.

There I was cruising through the madness and magic of Mumbai traffic accompanied by this boy who spoke half Marathi, half English.

So the boy tells me he is a magician. I think he is joking, or it's a pick-up line. It turns out he was not. For the next 15 minutes of our shared ride, he stole my heart with his fine mastery of coin magic. Instead, he was using rings: mine and his.

With his words, demeanour and tricks, he cast a spell and dragged me into a world of awe as our driver cut through cramped cars, once in a while stealing a moment to glance at us. He was for sure fascinated by our playfulness. I remember laughing so hard that my belly hurt. I remember the magician sharing with me about his life as a street artist. And how the spark in his eyes lit up when he spoke of his dream to become the best magician Mumbai had yet to experience.

He briefly touched on the hardships of working in the streets as an artist. I noted a slight but not so significant dip in energy. Before he could get 'stuck there' he quickly shifted his energy. He shared why he loves magic, how its impact on humans moves him, and more of his high life aspirations.

In those few minutes, I momentarily forgot where I was, who I was, and what was troubling me. Even the insane Mumbai hooting stopped. Nothing else existed but a strange boy, vanishing rings, magic, and me.

When he jumped out, and I snapped back to reality, it hit me that in the moments we shared, time had stopped. And a gateway to infinite possibilities had opened. My misfortunes were gone. My cheer was back. And that Mumbaiker thrill was once again running through my veins like wildfire.

This chance encounter jogged my memory on the power of any given moment to alter our inner way of being and consequently how we experience life. Whether through our words, like how the magician carefully crafted the narration of his dreams and street experiences. Or by embracing the unexpected mystical events in our lives, the power to decide how we decipher our experiences lies in our hands.

However, the human in us is prone to hold such insights momentarily. Seasons later, I had forgotten this vital lesson. Until I had another occurrence to remind me, only this time the hard non-magical way...

A broken Bluetooth speaker

Every memorable revolution was triggered by a couple of thought-provoking words and a handful of believers. Words can inspire us to move towards positive action or inflict turmoil that deters us from pursuing our goals. Think of a moment when a boss or colleague said something not so kind to you, and you walked around for weeks feeling 'terrible'. Looking back, you realise you lost precious time and energy that you could have channelled into other valuable pursuits.

Negative language can be hurtful when it's from others, but what about the language we use every day to label ourselves and describe our experiences? Isn't this negativity more disastrous?

One evening not so long ago, exhausted from dozens of work video calls, I decided to take a long hot shower while listening to some of my favourite jams. To pump me up, I brought my Bluetooth speakers to the bathroom. Fifteen minutes later (I know. I don't understand what y'all are doing in the shower for more than five minutes, so yes, fifteen was a real stretch), I was done.

Getting ready to leave, I picked the speaker and then momentarily placed it back just next to the sink, taking a minute more to tidy up my hair. Now, this is where the fun begins.

This action tripped the hand sanitiser bottle, which fell over, pouring its contents on the speakers. Speakers that I loved so much.

Everything unfolded quite fast. In between, as I tried to salvage my precious speakers, I heard a voice in my head say, "What the heck is wrong with you? Why do you keep doing such stupid things? Why are you so messy?"

As soon as these words left my subconscious, my whole life flashed in front of me.

"How many times have I used similar simple accidents to label or judge myself harshly?"

A lifetime of memories came crashing over me.

I was a little bit shocked, because duh, I am like the master of positive thinking, right?

Luckily I have been learning to grieve losses. Hence, though frustrated by the possibility of my speakers never working again, I didn't wallow in that moment. Gazing at the mirror, I realised how such an event could lead to a chain reaction of flawed thinking for the rest of my day. Our thoughts left to run the show can be viral.

This is how my movie would have played.

A simple accident like this happens for the one-hundredth time and then...angry that I, thanks to my clumsiness, just ended the life of my favourite speakers, concluding I will never learn to be more careful. Not to mention I had smashed my favourite mug and seriously knocked off my big toenail on my way out two days earlier. Something indeed must be seriously wrong with me.

All day long, I keep thinking about the accident and how I can't stop being clumsy. I walk around thinking something is wrong with me. Feel something is wrong with me. Start to believe something is really wrong with me. Act like something is wrong with me. Eventually, I become something that is wrong. As I approach my work with this energy, I create adverse outcomes. And the rest of my life is written as wrong simply because I forgot to close a sanitiser bottle tightly.

How ridiculous, right?

We may not realise or even want to admit that such moments, which in the large scheme of things are 'insignificant' and should therefore be regarded as such, can lead to an accumulation of unfair conclusions and negativity that is destructive to our self-esteem.

These labels and self-defeating energy don't serve our progress. We move around unknowingly, dumping bits and bits of it in our everyday encounters, our work-life being the largest receiving vessel. Eventually, these are written all over our lives. And they become the lens through which we see ourselves.

Raising our awareness and ability to capture negative self-judging moments instantly, refraining from the urge to judge ourselves, and reframing the meaning we attach to occurrences can positively influence how we experience our career journeys.

Magical Triple Ts

Now I can imagine you've probably not sat through Mumbai traffic or any other traffic with a magician. But perhaps you've watched a magician perform?

If you haven't, please go ahead, keep this book aside, and give a few videos online a visit.

Don't you love that exhilarating feeling that builds up as your heartbeat accelerates? Your anticipation intensifies. Your hair rises with excitement as you watch the magic unfold.

You know, without a doubt, the magician is playing tricks on your brain. But you allow yourself to play along anyway. Oh, wait, so who is in control here? As the magician's performance unfolds, the suspense, charisma, wonder, and the unbelievable draw your attention into an infinite world of possibilities. Momentarily your perception of what is real and true is challenged. The mental obstacles you hold hang loosely. At some point, you may convince yourself their magic is real. And it is real. It is 100% magic, after all.

Great magicians spend most of their lives mastering one thing; getting exceptional at misdirecting our attention. A skill, when successfully utilised, helps us transcend our noisy, logical, and often negative minds. In those microseconds, when our attention is safely somewhere else, the magician reveals yet another trick. Once again, drawing us to commune with them in child-like awe-filled universes. I love magicians because they remind us of our innate core spirit. We are happy and free-minded beings.

It's just that, swallowed in our busy professional lives; we sometimes forget our sense of wonder.

I am convinced we need more magical misdirection in our careers. We spend too much time and energy focused on 'all the things going wrong'. And there is always a lot to find there when we look for it.

We need an overwhelm of beautiful distractions from the mundane, frustrating, and volatile world of work to reignite the magic that lies within each of us. Magical thinking can help us shift the negative and degrading perceptions we hold of ourselves.

However, we must remember it takes time, practice, and dedication to achieve mastery.

Many of the professionals I support are on various transition journeys to reclaim the forgotten magic in their lives. We spend several hours on language. Reframing every negative and demeaning thought or label that clouds their greatness. As a result, hindering them from progression. It's mesmerising to see how their inner and eventually outer world rapidly transforms when they flip how they perceive and speak about their career experiences.

I like to call these shifting sessions Magical Triple Ts - Thought Tweak Trick. In psychology, it's reframing.

Magical Triple Ts in action

"We are God's masterpiece..." apostle Paul wrote to the Ephesians. Whenever I contemplate this Bible verse, I cannot help myself from wondering: "What could the human race accomplish if our self-perception, our thoughts, and actions were guided by this belief?"

We are a masterpiece.

How delightful would it be to navigate our career misadventures, seek new opportunities, and elevate our performance while demonstrating a high regard for ourselves through our language?

Unfortunately, many professionals don't hold themselves this way, especially when their efforts hit the wall. Drawing from the countless career conversations I have had, I am confident that *tuning up the awareness of the impact of our language is an emergency.*

Let's explore how such awareness combined with playing Magical Triple Ts has previously shifted my clients' career experiences.

Instead of saying "I am the problem", we tweak to "I am a perfect human being just the way I am" or if that makes you feel a little arrogant or egocentric, perhaps something like "Even if there are things about me that are not yet perfect, that doesn't make me a problematic human being". Or: "There is a problem in how I am approaching my career, I need to find out which of my ways are generating the opposite results of what I wish for".

When our careers face roadblocks (notice *not us* facing roadblocks. Same situation, different description, therefore different impact on our psyche), we are inclined to conclude we are the problem. With time, we find all reasons to justify why we are the problem. Soon enough, the chain reaction kicks in. Gradually we forget our incredible abilities and successes. We are crippled by powerlessness while all we need is a hand to guide us through the unchartered waters.

"I will never make it" pops up when we feel we've tried almost everything possible to elevate our careers, and yet we bear no favourable fruits. Instead, we tweak this to, "I have accomplished impossible goals in the past. This is another uphill climb along the journey." And it is! In most cases, one has forgotten how they smashed some audacious goals just a few months ago.

"Why am I so useless?" comes up often when we make frequent mistakes or act in ways we believe others would disapprove of. The more we replay this statement, the more helpless we feel. How about, "My mistakes do not define me. This experience has taught me valuable lessons. I believe I have immense value to offer once I am in the right organisation/opportunity that values my potential".

Someone says, "You didn't approach your work thoughtfully". While deep down, you know you burnt the midnight oil to bring the project to light. However, you take these words to mean, 'you are not good enough or are incapable'. You walk in this spirit all day and approach your work feeling incapable. Before you know it, your results are unthoughtful. Consider flipping how you perceive the situation. "I did my best to deliver this task. It seems, though, there are few expectations I may have missed out on. I will purpose to find out what these are so I can sharpen my skills in this area"

Play with these simple tweaks and observe how your attention shifts to more forward-thinking action. You will notice a sense of relaxation and calmness enter your life, making you more grounded. You will slowly build the courage to navigate the unexpected challenges in your career. As you begin to alter your language positively, your thoughts and feelings also upgrade. This shift propels you to move boldly in creating the career you want and deserve.

As you welcome and settle into this new way of being, your renewed actions will create new outcomes. You will notice a remarkable shift in how you approach your job search, respond to job application regrets, an angry boss, a malicious colleague or a rejected promotion request. You will move gracefully through long and frustrating interview processes. Delayed feedback will not hold you hostage. Your muscle for meeting career obstacles cool-headed will have begun to take shape.

I am not asking you to become an overly optimistic false-positive thinker. I only recommend giving this idea of tweaking how you describe your experiences a try. Walk around for a day, intentionally watching your viral thoughts, notice how you describe situations and how that makes you feel. Hold space for unexpected realisations and emotions. And then get to the work of tweaking your perspective of each situation. No judgment. No spirals. If your tweaked views bring you sorrow after a day, then, by all means, consider this the worst suggestion ever.

In the long term, tweaking gives you a more profound sense of inner control over your career circumstances. Your muscle of 'I got this' strengthens. External and unexpected events no longer keep you from progressing. Like with the art of developing any habit, patience, time, and practice are a necessity for a long-term and sustainable impact.

Perhaps time and patience are not your styles. You prefer a more radical, drastic approach that snaps you out of your constant self-sabotaging and judgy viral thoughts. You are exhausted from all this negative self-labelling.

You want to win the invincible war of your thoughts fast and easy. I can share an approach I often use that has been quite impactful. I summon all the love, kindness, and authenticity within me and tell my mind to "Shut the F*&* Up". And then I dive straight into the deep end of whatever it is I was supposed to be doing in the first place.

Intention fans your magic

When we experience this 'I am stuck in my career feeling', we might feel like we want to run. Run towards being someone else. Escape the mundane. Get a new job asap. We are ready to start all over again. Dive into experiencing life opposite of how we've known it.

Simply put, we crave magic.

Our cup of awe is empty. Our spirit longs for a refill. In such moments, how might we cultivate and reignite the wonder and sensational living in our careers?

First, we must begin by revisiting and clarifying what it is we desire to achieve. And why we desire that. We must get utterly honest with ourselves about the true intentions of why we work. And what success uniquely means to us. Moreover, like the magician in Mumbai, we must embrace intention as our guiding star in our career decisions. Why am I really doing this? Will this path bring me magic or misery?

To intend is to purpose. Aim for something. Resolve to focus your attention and energy on creating what your heart truly desires. When we live true to our hearts, magic can never escape us.

When you approach your life, career, and relationships intentionally, you give the highest form of attention to the life unfolding in front of you. You see the call in every moment clearly. All your actions and thoughts are channelled towards responding clear-headed and mindfully to that call.

To intend is to focus with our whole being, deeply in the present moment, that no opportunity goes unnoticed. We do so because we know magic is everywhere. And often hidden in unexpected places.

To intend is to love. To love you. To love your goals. To love the process. To love the results. It's to love deeply everything you choose to pursue and engage in. Pure intention is free of the clutter of negative thoughts and takes purposeful action that leads us to pure outcomes.

The intentional one is committed to something that moves and inspires them greatly—something like the magic that lies within each of us.

An invitation to you:

How might allowing the power of intention into your life fan the magic in your career?

How could the spirit of intentionality help you move more strategically in your career?

A magical challenge for you

Over the next seven days, choose to bring all your attention to every word that rolls over and leaves your tongue. Become aware and take into account the frequency at which you use words or phrases that label you in a negative or demeaning manner.

Whenever such a realisation pops up, first take three deep breaths. Then tweak the specific language and thoughts.

Observe how differently you feel.

Take a moment to record both the demeaning language and your realisations from the tweaking exercise.

At the end of the week, evaluate your notes. What are the common threads of the phrases and words that lower your spirit and vibration? What did you learn from shifting your perspective in different moments?

Evaluating ourselves this way is not always easy. Be gentle with yourself. Commit to holding a safe space for yourself and restrain from further judgment. You've done that for far too long.

Play this challenge for a month. Then pause and look back.

What has shifted in how you show up? What feels different now about your current career realities?

Chapter 9

WHAT GODMOTHER UNIVERSE WANTS YOU TO FOCUS ON

"Pleasure in the job puts perfection in the job". Aristotle

The godmother universe's blunder

Once upon a time, the godmother universe (or whatever force made us possible) thought it was wise for each human to contribute uniquely to keep the mother earth breathing and thriving.

How marvellous would it be for individuals to show up undisguised, as their natural, authentic selves, dancing to their own rhythm and, together, co-creating the world they want to live in?

Hence, the godmother came up with the idea of talents, gifting us in different and valuable ways. In her grand master plan, each individual would grow and thrive in certain environments better than others. Consequently, they would catalyse growth and progression in various spaces (work, society, family, etc.).

Up to this moment, the game plan was perfect. Give us unique ways of being and scatter us like seeds across mother earth in environments that would allow us to grow, co-create and thrive. Confident she had it all figured out, the godmother universe went back to doing the other thing she does best, enjoying life.

Unfortunately, she forgot to include clear instructions on who was to fall where, and so the process of placing us on earth went haywire. Some of us landed on the wrong grounds. Sandy soil, rocks and thorny bushes. These grounds would thwart our efforts and our ability to grow naturally, use our talents, and maximise our limitless potential to flourish.

And so here we are. Dropped into the cosmos without a manual to tell us what conditions are favourable for us to unleash and grow our talents. What we are particularly good at, and how we can bring this to fruition. As a result, we spend most of our professional lives trying to figure out, mostly on our own, for what grounds we were initially designed.

In our careers, these grounds take different forms. In addition, they significantly influence how pleasurable our job experiences are and, in turn, our productivity and level of fulfilment. Grounds could be the type of tasks and responsibilities we carry out in our jobs or specific social causes and passions we feel called to pursue. They are also the type of work environment we find ourselves in: including colleagues, bosses, organisational policies, management approaches, etc.

When we 'feel stuck', notably, one of the key reasons is because we are on the wrong ground. A job that is not a good fit for our talents and strengths, or a job that is not a good fit for our passions and interests. In other cases, we find ourselves in the perfect role, but our playground (work environment) restrains us from showing up fully as the best version of ourselves.

Thus, it's crucial when this 'feeling stuck' arises; one takes it as an opportunity to reevaluate their 'day-to-day work tasks curiously. The aim of this is to pick up clues on the root cause of one's misalignment. The closer one gets to determining what type of work the godmother intended them to do, the faster they can identify the contrary aspects of their current job that make them feel stuck.

Perhaps it's a shift in the level of complexity. Thus, one is quickly bored and looks for the next challenge. Other times, the organisation's priorities have shifted, changing the 'spirit or approach' needed to deliver the work.

For example, I've had conversations with project managers who enjoy project management roles but become 'disconnected with their work' somewhere along the way. "I am not sure if these are strengths anymore, but I love and am great at project management," they frequently claim. At first, this is confusing. On further exploration, we find out that the nature of their job has shifted to external-facing activities such as facilitation and training. This involves lots of people facing work. Still, they would rather spend 70% of their time in the backend, developing systems to support project delivery and monitoring.

This chapter broadly explores simple techniques that can help us discover our talents, hidden strengths, and unique ways of contributing. The clearer this is to us, the more empowered we are to move boldly to spaces or grounds that allow us to thrive. And the easier it is to spot signs when things are off. In addition, we will look at how to enhance our performance by maximising our strengths and paying attention to our energy states.

Why simple techniques? Often, even well-researched scientific assessments miss the mark, as asserted several times by professionals that I've interacted with. Some are confused by the conflicting results from different tests. In other cases, it's difficult for individuals from certain parts of the world to relate to various assessment tools.

The truth is, we know ourselves best. Unfortunately, we are so preoccupied with our daily work lives that we rarely pay attention to how our lives are unfolding. Preoccupied with doing things, the revelations of our strengths and magic bypass us.

The techniques shared here take us back to the basics. Shut the noise and listen. What do you know to be true about your super abilities?

Actually, why don't you try that right at this moment?

Why we are talent shy

It's no secret that we crave the freedom to be ourselves. Free as we are to give our very best to life. The more one utilises their strengths and talents, bringing their magic and spice unafraid, the more satisfying and pleasurable their work (and life) becomes. Sadly, arriving at this place is a dream for various reasons.

First and foremost, our exposure limits us. For many of us, we have access to a few (relatable) role models who have made it by pursuing their talents and uniqueness. And those who are in our line of sight are frequently out of the way. Though their experiences stimulate our curiosity, their context and paths feel impossible for us to relate to, leaving us with limited tangible examples to model. Moreover, we are quick to distance ourselves from the handful who have followed their talents by easily labelling them as risk-takers or the lucky ones. In reality, it's their advantage of exposure, which provoked and shifted how they perceived their growth and development journeys.

Secondly, it's no surprise to meet professionals who can't outrightly and confidently tell you what they are good at. For these, contributing powerfully through their strengths is out of the question. When our ability to observe and listen to ourselves is deficient, it's hard to honestly and fully account for our talents and how our unique approaches add value.

Furthermore, our workplaces shape our levels of awareness by instituting systems that impede our ability to seek and provide conscious feedback. Other factors that limit the clarity of our strengths in our workplaces include: our best ally, the ego, who is committed to preserving our self-protection tactics; and our circles (read: your colleagues, managers, etc.) who care little about our growth, thus suppressing the emergence of our gifts.

This is a double-edged sword because we are too preoccupied with our own career interests to pay attention to and recognise others' emerging talents or spend five minutes fanning them when we notice them. Besides, how many professionals have you met who want to see you truly shine? Your answer is as good as mine.

Fear of the unknown or failure and spending too much time in our comfort zone are two other factors that prevent us from becoming aware of our talents, strengths, and gifts. With the former, one may know what they are good at but is too freaked out to step into it. While the latter keeps one safe doing the ordinary, prohibiting opportunities for their strengths from emerging.

Only genuine feedback and attention to what feels true to us will save us from wasting our gifts and talents. By the time we realise this, we are too deep into covering the gems within that turning back feels like diving into the ocean's deep without diving gear. So we abandon the idea altogether and settle on making the best of what we have. At the same time, we watch our talents and aspirations of what we could become waste away.

However, our calling always haunts us. It doesn't matter what age you are or how many ladders you've climbed in your career. I remember being ten years old, writing poems and song lyrics for my classmates, and secretly hoping to be an author one day. It only took me two more decades to step up, but the burning desire to work on my craft and to use this talent to serve, though lying dormant for so long, never ran out.

Our strengths, talents, the things we are really good at, the work put in our hearts, and our ways of contributing to the continuation of the universe will never escape us. They lie silently in us, waiting for a trigger for their awakening. Sometimes it's a grand life disaster, a middle life crisis or exposure to new ways that inspire a shift in our perceptions. When the moment is ripe, we fully embrace what we are good at without fear of being judged or failing. Because we can't really fail at pursuing what we already are.

The Limitless Potential Paradox

Once, I was facilitating a group coaching session. A participant asked, "So are you insinuating that we should focus solely on our strengths as our way of contributing and adding value to the organisations we work for? Doesn't that conflict with the idea of growth and stretching out of our comfort zone? What about my weaknesses? Should I stop working on developing my skills in these areas?"

"Great questions," I responded. Then proceeded to acknowledge her ten key strengths.

"Now tell me, have you mastered everything humanly possible in each of these incredible strengths you have? And if you say yes, aren't you declaring that you've reached the limit of your abilities? At this moment, can you confidently say you are the best the world has seen in your areas of strength?

There was a long silence before he reluctantly nodded: "OK, perhaps you have a point."

And I do.

A paradox is sometimes painful to accept, but we must learn to live with it. I call it the limitless potential paradox. On the one hand, we possess the infinite potential to be anything and everything we aspire to be. To master as many skills and bodies of knowledge as we are curious. On the other hand, there is only so much of ourselves, our time and energy that we can squeeze into our fleeting lifespans. These conflicting ideas can sometimes hold us back from deciding where to focus our efforts or overwhelm us with the pressure to excel at everything. Since the latter is unachievable in one lifetime, we must deliberately choose our areas of focus.

Any day, I choose to immerse myself in my strengths fully and then crawl through the areas that aren't as natural for me, one at a time. Why? Life is short.

It's worth noting that using the word 'focus' here doesn't mean abandoning your many interests and talents. Or ignoring the critical skills you need to develop to level up your game. For the former, also known as multi-talented or multi-curious, the idea of putting aside all the many interests that make our lives pleasurable and exciting can be terrifying. Relax, I have got your back.

Instead, in this context, focus refers to one's ability to intentionally and calmly choose from their bucketful of interests what to engage in fully, for a determined period, while carefully balancing one's current realities and future aspirations. In this period, one directs all their attention, energy, and time to build mastery of specific skills and knowledge in the chosen areas. And in positioning oneself as a compelling value creator in these areas for their current or future employers. A few years down the line, one could get bored or curious about something else on their list. Then, calmly, one reprioritises their list and pursues the learning adventures that speak to their soul at this point in their journey. Suppose this is you. Over the years, you will have built a wealth of knowledge and expertise in several areas, giving you the unfair advantage of plugging and playing in diverse work contexts.

Reconciling with the paradox of limitless potential frees us from unnecessary worries such as:

- The anxiousness of not using all our gifts.
- The panic of never being able to do this or that.
- The haste of jumping from one area of interest to another without building depth in anything.

Instead, we focus on pursuing the minimum yet most impactful actions that accelerate our growth and achievement of our career aspirations.

The truth is, when we become terrific in specific tasks of our work, our career brand can't remain a secret.

> An invitation for you:
>
> Now that you are familiar with the limitless potential paradox, where have you been stretching your growth a little too much and need to go a little bit easy on yourself?
>
> What are the three areas of your work that you know (and you do!) give you pleasure, and if you put all of your efforts into them, you'll become an expert in those fields? What's holding you back from doing so?
>
> Do you have a wide range of interests? Your head can't stop buzzing with a list of endless exciting things you wish to pursue. Pause: if you narrowed it down to 2-3 of these areas for the next three years, how would your career evolve?

Your feelings are your strengths. Listen!

Rumi once said, "Everyone has been made for some particular work and the desire for that work has been put in every heart". Clearly, the godmother story must have existed way back in the 13th century.

Cumulative experiences in jobs misaligned with the particular work the godmother universe put in our hearts lead us to that 'I am stuck in my career feeling'. We feel stuck because, deep down, we know there is more to us than the mundane tasks overflowing into our lives. We sit anxiously through seasons of longing to do something different. Anything else but this. This persistent and strong nudge screams silently that our work is not what we are meant to be doing.

Sadly, many of us suffer far too long before we can accept that our work drains the life out of us. Our hearts stopped singing a long time ago, yet the 'work is great' greeting response hangs loosely on our tongues. In our wildest imagination, risking our paycheck is the worst thing that could happen. But is this worse than spending over half of our lives in jobs that steal our joy? For others, it's the fear of making a leap of faith or giving up after several attempts to transition (check out the Transition is not an Overnight Adventure chapter) to their ideal jobs.

Whatever one's reasons, they will eventually find themselves trapped by the constraints of making a living vs pursuing work aligned with their strengths and talents. If, at that moment, the pain of staying is beyond their limits, they surrender to their truth. They are in a job that doesn't do justice to their talents and expertise.

As defining and glorious as such a moment is, it takes self-trust and dedicated reflection to reach this level of clarity and ownership. Thus it's crucial to frequently create time to indulge oneself in this question: How might I consciously identify the particular work that allows me to express my unique gifts, expertise and strengths?

There is an easy answer here.

Feelings.

Now, before you think I am mad, play along.

We know it too well. That draining feeling that arises when you are carrying out a task for five minutes, but it feels like you've spent your whole life doing it. Why does it never get easier? Though you've repeatedly engaged in this type of work, somehow, you feel emptied out every time. You are just not good at it. You've tried for many months or even years to feel any better when pursuing such tasks, but very little changes. Every time you jump into it, no matter how excited and energised you initially are, you end up feeling like you arc on a steep uphill journey.

It's not a secret that you don't enjoy it.

You would rather be doing everything else but this. Unfortunately, everything else is not in your job description. So you stick to what has is handed down to you. Every time you accomplish a draining task, you steal the opportunity to dance around foolishly. Celebrate yourself, as you've just won the hardest battle in your life. And you have. The struggle was internal, against the specific work that the godmother universe had placed in your heart. You might have won, but you are exhausted.

This frustrating feeling that never goes away when you undertake certain types of tasks is a sign you should be doing less and less of such work. Trust it.

Meanwhile, in a parallel universe, which might as well be just across your desk, your workmate puzzles you. They have the exact job description as yours, identical work tasks, same work conditions, same boss. Yet contrary to you, they seem always to be deeply engrossed in their work, in a strangely positive and playful manner.

From where you stand, it's like they are not working at all.

You wonder whether anything on their to-do list ever gets done. Yet they graciously and effortlessly deliver exceptional results at what seems like light speed while looking jolly, calm and confident.

How can they always have their shit so together? How can they always be so energised by the same type of work that exhausts you?

You wish you could partake in their secret magical pill.

The good news is, there is no magical pill.

These individuals are simply in roles that align more with their natural inner way of being. They are not fighting with the current. They are not monkeys trying to swim. They are simply partaking in the particular work that the godmother universe intended for them in the journey of co-creation. They are drawn to this type of work and have become really good at it over the years. Thus, their work feels effortless and enjoyable. As Aristotle says, this "puts perfection on the job." That's why all other factors held constant; they are often highly productive and deliver outstanding results. While you're battling every day to achieve 'merely average results'.

Escape the trap of standardised job descriptions

In most cases, our careers unfold like this: we get our first job, build a few skills there, get promoted one level higher, build a couple of new skills and knowledge there, get a new job, move one step up and so on. A couple of years later, we've become what we do. We speak about our strengths and expertise based on the several bullet points we've accumulated on our resumes. When we randomly encounter a stranger who poses the question of our strengths and notice they are not in it for jokes, but are rather genuinely interested in understanding what we are good at, it feels like we've been caught off-guard. We need a minute (often more) to quickly skim through the bullets in our job descriptions to put the words together. And still, we sense a disconnect between what comes out of our mouths and what we really want to say.

You are probably nodding right now. Rarely, as we journey through our careers, snakes and ladders, do we pause and reflect on our emerging strengths, the skills we are deepening and the talents blossoming. Eventually we are trapped in seeing ourselves as our job descriptions indicate—forgetting all the juicy aspects that make us whole and unique individuals with a lot more to offer at work.

Take some time to reflect at the moment on this simple question. What are you really good at? Not what the online tests have told you. Not what your job description tells you you are hired to do. Not what everyone around you is trying to force you to believe you are good at.

What you know for sure. And you do.

Because you have experienced being good at it, you've enjoyed partaking in this type of work. You feel engaged, energised and alive when you undertake work of this nature. You move through it effortlessly and create remarkable results in short periods.

> What tasks are these for you? What makes you feel and look like your workmate in the parallel universe?

It's fascinating the way we humans, myself included, run away from our authentic selves. We know we're good at something. Heck, we've proven it to ourselves numerous times. But here we are, complicating things by continuing to indulge ourselves in tasks that bore us and squeeze life's enthusiasm out of us. Even when we get the chance to do something different, we choose safety.

Another way we run away from our greatness is by aiming to be an all-rounded professional and pursuing being good at everything, all at once. Technically, thanks to the limitless potential paradox, this is impossible. But we are stubborn beings, so we do so anyway, along the way, neglecting to go deep into anything. We spend less time investing in and mastering our unique gifts and talents that lie untapped in us. Our unevenly distributed efforts mould us into half-baked masters. In the end, we can do a lot of things well, but none of them greatly.

Now, I understand why organisations need these documents. But what restricts YOU from describing yourself, your abilities and your special sauce in potential job conversations without the soulless words in your job description? Words that only make sense in the organisational context of your employer?

In addition, it's not unusual to find that in many organisations, one's actual day-to-day work is beyond what is in their job descriptions. At other times, one is engaged in volunteer opportunities, hobbies, part-time roles in line with their interests, and nothing to do with our jobs. These all feed into our expertise. These exciting and valuable experiences that shape who we are and what we can deliver are often left out when we package our expertise.

Interviews are one fascinating space that keeps recruiters, and hiring teams entertained, if not overly frustrated. I've lost count of the number of times I've had to ask professionals to explain, as if to a 5-year-old, what their actual unique contribution to their roles is. As opposed to the robotic narration of the bullet points on their job descriptions. When they slow down and speak from their hearts unfiltered, what they share is more comprehensible and paints a compelling picture of how their skills and distinctive approaches come to play and create value.

In short, stop using the old, boring language in most of your job descriptions to speak about yourself, especially in your CV, cover letters and interviews. What is written there is probably outdated and an unfair representation of your abilities.

When you try to express yourself using other people's words, in this case, those in your job description, you must first agree with me that it is difficult to translate their words into your own meaning. And two, you miss the essence of your strengths, your uniqueness and your talents. Most 'official languages' lack that heartfelt connection that sparks enthusiasm about how you tell the story of your abilities.

How can we bring more spice to identifying and speaking about our core strengths, unique approaches, expertise, and how these create value for organisations?

You can try the fun exercise below.

Create your own strength's language

Forget momentarily, force yourself if you have to, your current job tasks, your previous and your desired future job. Forget all the vocabulary that describes what you do. Take those images of job descriptions stuck in the back of your mind and stash them in your box of forgetfulness.

Now, grab a pen and a piece of paper. Allow your mind to wander freely in no particular direction.

While at it, start reflecting and writing down what comes to mind when you think of the following questions.

Dreamland: Imagine you are now in your ideal role, where you are immersed most of the time in work that makes you feel fully engaged and energised. What tasks would you want to fill most of your day? How would your incredible workweek be scheduled?

You are in charge here, so dream away!

Now go one step deeper. Why did you choose these tasks? Evaluating each at a time, what do they tell you about your strengths and unique abilities? About work that brings you joy?

End of the world: The world is coming to an end, and each of us can only participate in two tasks to save humanity. Tasks that only we can do confidently well. Tasks that we trust we will not mess up. Because if they do, lives are at stake. What will you include on your list?

Play: Now, imagine yourself engaging in work that feels like play. You are dancing through your tasks and smashing those goals like a pro. You've got your act together, and you're excited and joyful about the work you're doing. Actually, this feels like no work at all.

What are these tasks? What are they signalling about your strengths?

Eyes closed trick: What type of work tasks can you do with your eyes closed if someone wakes you up at 3 a.m.?

Secret crush: What is the type of work you secretly wish you could do more of? You know you'd truly enjoy it and be more fulfilled if that was all you did for the rest of your life.

Your legacy: Finally, imagine that you've left an organisation that you served for 15 incredible years. You've built remarkable teams and created exemplary value for the organisation. What will the team left behind miss you for? What tasks will they wish they could find a clone of you for? Because no one, absolutely no one, can fill that gap? These are your unique ways of creating value.

Fantastic! How was this activity like for you? What are you realising about your capabilities and untapped potential?

Now compare what you discovered above to the tasks you are currently working on in your day-to-day job. How aligned (or mis) are you?

What shifts must happen for you to rise into roles that allow you to co-create with the godmother universe through your unique abilities? In a more pleasurable manner?

If you are currently looking for new opportunities, do the jobs you are considering and expressing interest in include 60-70% of what is on the list you just created?

If it helps you get your visualisation started, I am really good at my list of things. The stuff that the room misses when I bounce. The stuff I secretly wish I could do all my life. You can call me at 3 a.m., and I'll be ready to kick ass. The stuff that the godmother universe put in my heart.

Tasks that the godmother wants me to focus on

- Brainstorming
- Big picture visioning and strategising
- Connecting ideas, finding patterns
- Leading strategic conversations about anything, really
- Dreaming big and building a vision
- Simplifying complex ideas/problems
- Leading in chaos and thriving in uncertain times
- Solving any problem creatively.
- Curating exhilarating and transformational learning and fun experiences
- Hosting meaningful conversations
- Being so aware of the simple moment-by-moment life experiences and using them to draw and bring insights into humans' lives through writing and photography
- Creating out of the box strategies
- Making stuff up (creating from nothing)
- Influencing others to buy into a vision
- Listening with my whole being
- Holding space for others to be
- Building trust quickly

My role in the co-creation of a better planet demands that I tap these superpowers loudly, playfully, as often as I can in my work. I do this through multiple roles. As an entrepreneur, career coach, innovation management consultant, learning experience designer, recruiter, leadership development coach, teacher, events curator, writer, photographer, and many others yet to be explored.

When I fully contribute to these skills, I create results more efficiently and effectively. And yes, work is pleasurable!

Tasks that suck the life out of me

- Structuring things – this drove me to insanity while writing this book. I almost gave up writing it
- Making sense of complex data
- Managing projects
- Managing people - which is why I am building a self-governing team.
- Tracking activities leaves me feeling dead inside and like a terrible person.
- Networking with many new people, all at once.
- Engaging in conversations that lack vision or meaning
- Working on tasks that require a high level of detail.
- Everything that requires detailed planning
- Now, it's your turn to write and get clear about your thoughts, so you can dance!

Dancing with your strengths & 'weaknesses'

Achieving our career aspirations goes hand in hand with our ability to intentionally navigate and balance our strengths and 'weaknesses' gracefully and tactfully, like a dancer.

As much as we'd love to bask in the presence of roles that only require our strengths, feel effortless and allow us to create maximum value in short periods, we know that this dream world is far from existence. Few of us will have the luxury of working in roles that require 100% of our natural abilities and expertise. In most cases, we will need to learn to manoeuvre between roles that we find pleasurable and those that we don't. How we treat and respond to ourselves in such moments affects how we approach specific tasks and, as a result, our productivity.

Furthermore, the higher one climbs the ladder of seniority or shifts to a new profession, the more one is bombarded with tasks and roles that the godmother never placed in their heart.

Several times, clients have called me after starting a new job, their dream job for that matter. On the edge of quitting, they shower me with a brief, beautiful rant. "I didn't think my dream job would be this hard!" they exclaim. I smile, knowing that their journey out of their comfort zone is just getting started.

"It's not, you are just out of your normal playing ground", I responded.

So, yes, it's expected that we will, along the way, do work that feels pleasurable and work that drains us. How might we through these experiences gracefully and sometimes quickly, like a dancer, while maintaining our centre of gravity?

Let's explore.

Maximise awareness

Earlier, we discussed feelings as the signposts that raise your awareness of what you are good at and whatnot. When you maximise understanding and acceptance of your strengths and areas of struggle, you move along with less friction and more efficiently in figuring out your growth and development. Every feeling is a messenger drawing your attention to what to focus on, what to let go of and what to explore further. Stay aware of your enjoyable roles and those that are likely to fast-track you to the burnout zone. Not necessarily because you are doing too much of these. But because you are doing less of what sparks the light in you.

When you raise your awareness this way, the questions you ask as you review potential job descriptions evolve. For instance, you ask, "How will I feel when executing such tasks most of the time?" With potential employers, you are keen to know, "What will success look like within the first six to twelve months?"

Knowing the organisation's focus gives you a sense of the spirit required for the role, what most days will look like, and whether this is the type of work that is pleasurable for you.

Like everything else, tuning up your level of awareness is a practice whose muscles grow with time. Reflections and external honest feedback help by shining a light on your strengths. Here are a few exercises you can consider incorporating into your career journey.

The work pleasure diary

What work has gifted you with pleasurable feelings today?

Consider keeping a diary if you wish, for the next 30 or 60 or 100 days. Record every day at least one task that brings you joy. You enjoyed immersed in these. You loved the results you created. You wish you could only have just that on your desk every day.

In addition, record a few more tasks that felt like the complete opposite. What felt draining and frustrating? Not because you can't do it. You are perfectly skilled, actually, but this work drains the life out of you.

The Friends Circle Challenge

Step into this challenge with a curious and open mind.

The essence of this challenge is to uncover your hidden strengths and talents in a safe space.

Choose four to five people who have closely observed and engaged with you in your day-to-day work, as well as at least one person who has interacted with you in social settings.

Make sure the individuals you choose are people who you believe have your best interests at heart. Who believe in your potential and want you to blossom.

Invite your trusted circle of humans to reflect on the questions below. Then go for a date with each or all to capture their reflections. Listen with an open heart and a free mind.

- When I think of (insert your name), I see these three superhero traits/skills in them. And I've seen them come out in these situations.
- I think what (insert your name) should be doing more of is... They appear to enjoy it but don't get enough of it.
- If I had a magic wand, I would banish this type of (insert your name) day-to-day work. That stuff exhausts them!

As they share, take note of all the new insights and affirmations that come up. Ask further questions to *understand how they see you when you don't see yourself*. Stay curious and open-minded to soak in everything magical about you!

Begin to master your energy

Remember the limitless potential paradox?

Let me refresh your mind.

Humans have infinite potential but are limited by our earthly lifespan, time and energy (physical, emotional and mental). In short, there is a limit to how far we can push ourselves without breaking down.

Coming back to the mystical world of dancers. To have a long, fruitful and fulfilling career, a dancer must master using their energy efficiently. Professional dancers will sometimes work eight to twelve hours, non-stop, every day. This, without doubt, stretches every single cell in their bodies and leaves them exhausted. That is why resting for exemplary dancers is a mandatory requirement. A great dancer can't afford burnout. Neither can you.

Dancers know it's in the resting period when their muscles grow stronger, their moves sink into their subconscious, and their energy builds up. Rest is a prerequisite for success. When the time comes for them to take their place on the stage and shine, they are fresh, energised, empowered to deliver a magical performance—leaving us all stunned.

If you want to build momentum by delivering consistent, incredible work results in your career, learn how to be a successful dancer.

Adopting rest is one way to model the ways of a dancer. In this context, the rest takes two forms. One is the literal meaning of 'resting' and doing nothing (it's OK if you are still settling into this idea). Or shifting one's attention to their hobbies or family connection time. These activities rejuvenate and build up our physical and mental energy. The other is rest from tasks that drain our energy, thus exhausting us, suck the excitement out of us or take forever to get done. The more we engage in such roles, the further we walk away from high levels of productivity. Thus, we must learn to consciously partake in these in small doses and, two, know when we've reached our maximum limits, and it's time to plug out.

The most obvious path to bringing the ways of a dancer into your career is to integrate dancing into your workout routine or work breaks, especially after exhausting tasks. Dance relaxes and loosens the tension in your body (and we build a lot of stress when we engage in work misaligned with our strengths). Dancing also connects you with your positive spirit, leaving you more grounded (we often feel disconnected when we perform tasks that drain us). In the long run, dance chases away the unavoidable bad vibes along your path. This helps if your boss enjoys throwing your way the worst of tasks. In such moments, you can dance yourself back to a state of relaxed focus and productivity.

If these reasons are not moving you to dance or in case right about now you are freaking out about your two left feet, relax, my friend.

Dancing here includes turning the volume of your favourite songs up, allowing the music vibrations to massage your heart and bones until you can't help yourself jumping around freely in your lawn or bedroom.

Through dance, we learn to embrace and flow with the yin and yang of pleasurable and unpleasurable work. We learn to move through our strengths powerfully and our weaknesses gently. When we dance through our tasks, which we can literally do, we surrender to the moment and take advantage of every opportunity to create a masterpiece in our work.

Along with dancing, strive to embody simple techniques that you can use in your daily life to manage your energy and maintain your grace.

Think through your schedule in energy terms. When am I most clear-minded, fresh, energised and with the least distractions? What tasks require most of my energy and attention, thus best plugged in at this time of the day?

What tasks drain my energy the most? How might I sandwich these between other tasks that make me feel alive to balance my productivity?

What tasks feel pleasurable and effortless to me? It doesn't matter when or where I am, I can tune in to get them done instantly? How do I best allocate these throughout my week, so my days have frequent moments of pleasure?

What fun activities (including dancing) do I need to incorporate into my breaks, especially after a long, tasking, and energy-draining task?

And finally, what is one insight you've realised from the successful ways of a dancer you'd love to incorporate into your career moving forward?

Over to you. What precisely will you try out tomorrow?

Grow one unpleasurable skill at a time

I get it.

You are ambitious.

You want to explore your limitless potential.

You have dozens of skills and knowledge you want to master.

Several of these are likely in areas that are not so pleasurable for you.

But hey,

Getting out of your comfort zone is your way of being.

For you, growth is inevitable.

Overwhelm, on the other hand, is avoidable.

Often, on our fast track to advancing our careers, we can get caught up in deciding what new skills to learn. It's human to want to learn a variety of skills and knowledge. Hesitate from the trap of pursuing learning paths that do not matter in the long run or are completely misaligned with what the godmother wants you to focus on.

Other times, when an individual can not create time and space to pursue their learning objectives or sees others moving faster than they are, it's easy to worry about lagging.

To keep yourself off these traps, consider reflecting on the following.

How then do you pick and prioritise your learning and development focus areas without overburdening yourself, especially with less pleasurable skills for us? Consider asking yourself these five questions.

Urgent & detrimental? Is my career advancement at high risk if I don't develop myself to at least a minimum level in these skills? Is my ability to contribute to my field endangered if I don't cultivate these mindsets in the shortest period?

Is this area necessary for my long-term success? Carefully consider your highest career aspirations. Do you really need this skill or knowledge to succeed at that level if you're completely honest with yourself? Examine other successful people to see if they use this skill or knowledge. If the answer is no, drop it.

What will my industry or profession need 5, 10 years from now?

Your investment in your learning and development should prepare you to be future-ready in your own space.

Is this a pretty add-on? Or rather, is it nice to have skills or knowledge that make you look polished but will not add any monetary value or opportunity for unique exposure? If it is, drop it.

Is someone working on a robot that will do this better than humans in a few years? Forget learning it. In the meantime, until the skill is fully automated, consider outsourcing.

This exercise helps you narrow down your long list of unpleasurable skills to what you must cultivate to get ahead. From here, prioritise your learning journey based on what is urgent and crucial for your most immediate goals.

For the skills that have a long-term impact, purpose to develop these at a steady pace—taking into account time, energy, and investment costs.

A robust value creator is excellent at what they do. Thus, focus on one unpleasurable area at a time, become great at it and then pick another.

Ultimately, the most crucial role you play in your career journey is to remain conscious of how your talents and gifts are unfolding. The more mindful you are in observing how you feel in diverse tasks and roles, the more you sharpen your awareness of where your sweet spot lies. And from here, you can groom and maximise these to:

- Bring more pleasure into your work life.
- Create value for organisations naturally.
- Tap into your infinite potential

Chapter 10

OWNING YOUR WORTH

You can know you are capable but not own your abilities. You can know your worth but not own your worth.

Ever been recognised for being exceptional in certain traits but felt disconnected from them? "Oh is that really me?" You may have responded for the 100th time—a sign you've not wholly owned all of you.

Owning all of you moves you towards your extraordinary. You boldly take your space. You confidently proclaim your worth. You are unapologetic about the terms you accept in exchange for your time, expertise, and energy.

Body-wise speaking

We possess so much magic within us. If only we could own just a fraction of it.

To own is to acknowledge something is true as we have experienced it. What we own, we can claim. For it belongs to us. Ownership gives us the power to go all the way in our pursuits.

Though today I am obsessed with the idea of owning every damn thing that we carry in our bones, souls, hearts, skin and all, I wasn't always like this. Until a few years ago when I attended a body intelligence workshop. And my whole world was flipped upside down.

Body intelligence focuses on the idea that our bodies are reservoirs of wisdom. If you find this unconvincing, perhaps a reminder that the elements of our bodies are made from leftovers of a supernova might help? Or that the human body is made up of roughly a hundred trillions fluid atoms? We are not even solid! So yeah, body-wise speaking, we humans are some really good stuff going on!

At the particular workshop, we were encouraged to move around freely. We danced intuitively, surrendering to the rhythmic call of the universe.

Like any other body intelligence class, we were then invited to notice what parts of our bodies felt constrained, heavy, unfree, painful, restricted, or discomfort. Once identified, we focused on the specific areas and became fully aware of the arising feelings.

The more one focuses on becoming aware and simply sensing and feeling, the more still their mind becomes.

And that is when things start to get interesting. With this new level of awareness, the facilitator prompted further: "As you notice that tight or constrained feeling in your body, curiously ask, what are you here to remind me of?"

Yes, it's a bit weird if it's your first time in such a workshop. You are tempted to think you are crazy. Relax, we all are. Who are you speaking to? Can your body even listen? At first, you doubt it. Then you are encouraged to trust the process, and when you do, something miraculous happens.

I quickly became aware of the tightness at the back of my neck, just next to the throat chakra (energy centre). The throat chakra helps us express our truth freely and authentically.

When it's open and healed, we communicate openly, honestly, and truthfully. We are honest with ourselves and others. When the opposite is true, we feel anxious or afraid of expressing our honest thoughts, ideas, or opinions with others.

Ever felt like you want to say something, but there is this lumpy, thick feeling in your throat holding your words back? For instance, when you want to call out a colleague or a family member or a friend for something that feels misaligned with your vibes, but instead you keep it within? Exactly. This is a sign that your free and authentic energy centre is blocked.

Back to my workshop. When I asked the question, "What are you here to remind me?"

The wisdom download came fast and strong.

"To own fully who you are.".

"To surrender to your true essence".

"To own your voice".

"To relax into your greatness".

"To listen even more deeply to your inner wisdom".

"To love more deeply the magical being you are".

At first, I thought, "What nonsense is this? Am I not one of the most authentic humans walking on the planet right now? I mean, what else do you want from me, universe?"

Reading my thoughts, she was quick to respond, "Trust the process," the facilitator channeled the message. "Your body is a carrier of a wealth of wisdom".

As I received more downloads, I slowly realised that I had only scratched the surface of my authenticity.

I couldn't wait to explore and find out what else of my power, magic, and authenticity I was yet to own. What greatness was silently waiting to be awakened. And what aspects of my voice I could have been silencing.

That same week, as I reflected and explored this new awareness further, I coincidentally noticed the similarities of these two words.

Owning & Knowing

(You see it too, right?)

You can KNOW your VOICE but not OWN your VOICE

You can KNOW you are CAPABLE but not OWN your ABILITIES

You can KNOW you are TALENTED but not OWN your TALENTS

You can KNOW Your SELF-WORTH but not OWN YOUR WORTH

You can KNOW your BELIEFS and VALUES but not OWN them in your day to day ACTIONS

You can KNOW YOURSELF but not OWN WHO YOU ARE

You can KNOW you are BADASS but not OWN your BADASSERY

You can KNOW your UNIQUENESS but not OWN your UNIQUENESS

You can KNOW you are BEAUTIFUL but not OWN your BEAUTY

You can KNOW you are HANDSOME but not OWN your HANDSOMENESS

You can KNOW you are EXTRAORDINARY but not OWN your EXTRAORDINARINESS

You can KNOW you are GIFTED but not OWN your GIFTS

You can KNOW you are AMAZING but not OWN your AMAZING TRAITS

You can KNOW you are WORTH MORE but not OWN your WORTHINESS

You can keep adding your OWNs.

I shared this with a couple of people in my circles, and many thought it was profound. I KNEW it was PROFOUND; their acknowledgement made me OWN its PROFOUNDNESS.

Suppose you've had people say great things about you or openly compliment your exceptional traits in the past. You are beautiful. You are outstanding. Your work is exemplary. You are so kind. Yet in those moments, you felt a disconnect between their words and how you felt within, you know you are all these things, but you don't feel like it in your bones and soul, then you know what I am speaking about.

This distinction of owning vs knowing has a massive impact on our careers. We may know our abilities from what we hear from others and what we see in our work results and yet, for various reasons, not own any of it. We walk around dismissing ourselves as we are tuned out of our amazingness.

I am inviting you to pause and reflect. In what ways in your career is this distinction of knowing vs owning currently playing out?

To own is to Wabi Sabi

Ownership is a hard call. It pushes us to embrace our Wabi Sabi, the Japanese concept of imperfection. Ownership is equivalent to radical acceptance. Flaws, cracks, rot, doubts, scars, fears, imposter syndrome, uneven body parts and all.

For many of us, even one dot of 'the unacceptable' can disconnect us entirely from everything else that is good within us.

Wabi-Sabi encourages us to love imperfection. For it is our imperfect that makes us unique and brings our authenticity to life. The Japanese culture honours flaws so deeply that broken pottery is mended with gold.

There is a Japanese legend that emphasises this concept. Once a young man named Sen no Rikyu went on an adventure of discovering the hidden gems behind the Japanese Tea customs. Sen was keen to learn from the best; thus, he apprenticed with a tea-master named Takeeno Joo.

Now, Takeeno was a wise man. When Sen showed up, he asked him to partake in some gardening activities. Sen went ahead to sweep the garden until it was sparkling clean meticulously. And then he did the unimaginable. Before asking his master to assess his work, he intentionally shook a cherry tree painting the spotless ground with a few flowers. Now it was perfect.

This is a complex concept for many of us to grasp. Yet without complete acceptance (especially of our flaws), we hold ourselves back from fully owning our magic, showing up in our world of work glamorously dressed in it, and taking our space at the stage to share our magic and worth with the world.

Whether you are seeking a new job opportunity or transitioning from one phase or profession to another, ownership will go a long way in boosting your confidence. When you own your value and come to peace with the fact that not all roles allow you to shine, you slay through job assessment conversations like the extraordinary, capable, talented value creator you are. Show up in any other way, and you are destined to sell yourself short.

To reach this place of harmonious and complete ownership, one must do the uncomfortable work. The work that clears the masks that hide our magic. A lot of this is discussed in various chapters in this book. To bid farewell to unuseful modesty, let go of the no-sense in our heads, hold space for growth and unshackle ourselves from the dead-end stories that keep getting in the way of our success.

The result of this is an increased ability to express ourselves freely, authentically and confidently. We can serve unafraid of contributing uniquely, speak our truth and boldly ask for what we deserve. You'd say at this point, your throat chakra is finally open.

You must create time now and then to evaluate, "What right now could be holding me back from owning my fabulous magical self?"

Cultivating such a practice increases the chances of spotting the little lying voices that unknowingly creep up. Consequently, creating the opportunity to smash these before they accumulate and overly cloud your judgement of your abilities.

And yes, it's an extra cherry on top to hire a coach to support you in mastering the artful way of packaging your experiences. Activities such as crafting a great resume, sharpening your interview hacking skills and developing a compelling pitch are essentials that enhance your external brand.

Finally, you should care about your state of ownership because it's not the job of potential employers to struggle in figuring out what you are truly made of. Or whether you are convinced you can do the job fantastically. It's your job to show them quickly and effectively that you are their best bet. Your ability to communicate and demonstrate this unfolds like child's play when you fully step into owning you, beauty, cracks, and everything.

Your career worth in a formula

How do I package my worth to employers?

How do I demonstrate that I can truly create value for the organisation?

I have over 15 years of work experience. How do I summarise all my incredible experiences to demonstrate I have what it takes to deliver beyond expectations?

Do my qualitative attributes matter more than my skill-set and quantitative results?

I have barely worked for more than three years. Am I even worth anything, or is every job a learning opportunity? (Wrong).

What if I am underselling myself? Great question, you probably are.

Sadly, no one asks, "What if I am overselling myself?" The cause of all headaches for hiring teams. Luckily, this book is not about them.

No matter what stage you are at in your career, the question of how much your accumulated expertise is worth is unavoidable. Even entry-level graduates are expected to show how they can create value.

Therefore, one needs to step into job conversations, having embraced the mindset of a value creator. Often in our day-to-day lives, we don't think of ourselves this way. Instead, questions of worth and value creep right back into our minds when we begin seeking a career move.

Caught unprepared, we rush to package our expertise. Unsure if we are doing it right, we hurriedly hire a coach, hoping that they can miraculously help us 'build our career brand' overnight. With little time to internalise and own our worth, we end up generating unnecessary doubts. This prevents us from communicating our abilities compellingly and confidently, asking for what we want.

Oh, how we wish there existed a walk-in valuation centre offering stamped certificates indicating our worth and an estimate of our compensation level. Come to think of it, that would be freaking amazing. Saving both employers and professionals the time and energy wasted playing mind games with each other.

Seeing competent professionals undersell themselves pains me. In contrast, I find engaging with ego-inflated individuals with little results to show but high compensation demands perplexing.

Ultimately, every job seeker needs to remember that employers only want to know three things as complicated as the job assessment processes. Can you offer the value my business requires? Can you do this job well? And while at it, can you manage to adapt smoothly and efficiently to meet the shifting business demands?

Unfortunately, many of us get things slightly twisted. We confuse our professional worth with our overall self-worth. Instead of simply keeping our focus on clearly demonstrating we can deliver the job exceptionally well, we get caught up in the rabbit hole of doubting if we can do the job. Yet, our past proves we can. As a result, we end up projecting the doubt instead of our track record of success. Doubt shows up in how we speak about ourselves, the terms and conditions we negotiate for, how we push back when our demands are not met, and so on.

Moreover, the lack of a structured approach for communicating the sum of our worth and aligning our expertise with the organisation's vision and goals troubles many of us.

Let's consider a systematic, organised formula that can help you compellingly package your competence without leaving the critical aspects unmentioned.

Your past relevant accomplishments/ successes + your capabilities (Strengths, gifts, talents, superpowers, how you uniquely add value, knowledge, and skills you've mastered) + Your proven ability to stay agile = Your Worth/ Value

Simple right? You already know all these things!

When using this formula, let's say in interview conversations or job applications, you have two objectives. One is to make sure that you bring out at 100% clarity each component of the formula. The other is to ensure you share nothing short of phenomenal examples of roles that have sharpened your relevant skills. When you share underwhelming examples, it is assumed you lack the depth and breadth required to hack the job at hand.

Finally, the PAR approach (as discussed in chapter 5) is helpful in structuring and communicating your outstanding work examples.

Keeping an account of your worth

It's ok. With all the buzz in our lives, keeping an account of your remarkable self is not often a key priority. Caught up in a rush for the next big thing, we forget to acknowledge our successes and document our unfolding strengths as much as we should.

However, what's not ok is to read the ideas below and refuse to make any tiny changes.

Once you've stepped fully into owning your worth, the next step is to start accounting for it. This ensures you are always armed with the very best and proudest examples of your experiences. As seen in the formula shared above, many aspects sum up your worth or value.

Imagine having an updated list of your baddest skills and strengths, your outstanding successes, your unique gifts, examples of how you've adapted and thrived in agile work environments, what you learned, the impact you created, etc. Don't you already feel more confident to go out there and hold exploratory job conversations?

Here are a few ideas to keep in mind in your accounting process.

Set the intention to remember

Believe me when I say you will forget the tiny significant details of your accomplishments. I know if I asked you right now to list your ten impressive work achievements from the last six months, your mind might go blank for a few seconds or even minutes.

It's the nuances of your experiences that carry the essence of your strategic, unique, and magical approaches. This is the stuff that makes you stand out in assessment processes. Unfortunately, caught in the hustle of your crazy world of work, you will forget those last-minute strategies and tweaks you initiated that, in the end, were the big breakthrough moments. As a result, you will show up for a job conversation and catch yourself several times saying, "I don't recall the details; it was a long time ago". The interviewer will nod their head and say it's ok. They will fake that they understand you. They don't.

Your responses lack substance. Without concrete illustrations, it's hard for an assessor to make a judgement on the depth and breadth of your experience, from which they approximate the quality and level of your skills. And so you receive a regret. It's nobody's fault. Things could have turned out differently if only you had remembered outstanding examples.

Many times I have heard clients exclaim after a deep dive coaching session, "Wow! I can't believe I had forgotten all these amazing things I have achieved in my career!"

To capture and communicate the essence of your accomplishments, talents, or competencies, always use the PAR approach to record your most significant moments.

Review your list often to remind yourself what an extraordinary human you are!

Your worth is not a secret. Speak it into the world

Nobody will know what you are made of until you speak and show it to the world. When you proclaim what you are and follow through with action, your colleagues and bosses start to associate you with your true essence. *Our words create our world.* Your spark, your greatness, your worth, your uniqueness, and all those little and big things that make you a remarkable professional can only be tapped into and utilised if they are known.

Now, I understand there is gospel out there of letting your actions (only) speak for you, and I am in full support. But I need you to remember, not many managers and colleagues are out there waiting to spot your magic so they can fan it.

So stop hiding. Stop hiding your expertise and uniqueness just because some tasks are not in your job description. Stop staying dumb about your successes. Talk about the tasks that excite you. Share your ideas about how particular challenges could be approached differently.

Does specific work make your heart dance? Put on your dancing shoes and take pleasure dancing through the task.

Did you recently realise you possess superhero skills in certain tasks? Share your aha moment with your colleagues.

Did you accomplish a significant goal lately? Talk about it in the next team meeting.

Have you recently mastered a new skill after putting in extra hours in the last couple of months? Share the joy of this milestone with someone.

Owning your worth is an everyday practice. When we speak out about the amazing things we are pursuing in our careers, they begin to feel real. Moreover, the more you speak something into the world, the more you act and become it. I believe you want to show up like your divine, worthy and outstanding self.

Consequently, showing up for interviews and other assessment processes becomes a natural process for you. You are simply dropping by to share what you already know and own.

Getting compensated for your worth

People ask me all the time how much they should ask for when the salary question comes up. Honestly, I don't know what you want to hear from me on this. My honest answer is, it depends. How much do you believe you are worth for the value you create?

Over the years, I have coined a couple of questions that have helped my clients figure their compensation expectations more strategically.

First, let me refresh your mind, how you got here. After freaking out about whether you can deliver the value the organisation requires and seriously stressing your heart out, sometimes you are lucky, and you receive a confirmation that the company would love to make you an offer.

Hurray! You celebrate for microseconds and immediately press a new stress button. This time on worrying about negotiating for the same value you initially doubted you were capable of delivering. It sounds ridiculous, you must agree.

As long as you exchange your time, energy and talents to deliver specific value for organisations, you commit to receiving money and other benefits in exchange. With this in mind, consider the following questions when preparing for compensation conversations with potential employers.

What do you want? And why do you want it?

Knowing what you want saves you from the trap of vagueness, indirectness and unwholly consideration of all benefits a job offers you.

As I continue to explore the hidden gems within me, the question of what I want and why has continued to haunt me. So if you are terrified right now for not knowing what the heck you want, worry no more. I promise not to bore you with an exercise to uncover your darkest desires.

Instead, I will engage you with a brief story about my daily struggles in distinctively what I want. I hope this helps!

Several months ago, I had this enlightening encounter on some of my true desires while shopping for a yoga mat. I had precisely 15 minutes to quickly drop by a household items outlet, pick up a new mat, and head to a nearby cafe to take a call.

Once I arrived at the mat section, I found myself staring at this gorgeous pink mat and thinking, "Wow, I love it! I have always wanted a yoga mat of this shade and texture".

Concurrently, a striking dark emerald greenish mat instantly drew my attention. Now, on some days I love elegant things.

I realised I was attracted to both. So now what?

I liked the elegance of the greenish one and the fact that it doesn't stain easily. (My zone of genius will never be cleaning).

The pink one, though, felt like my true calling. For the playful, creative, calm, harmony, the tenderness that I approach my workout routine with.

Surely I could afford both. Should I buy both? I wondered.

"Maybe not Martha, that's not in line with your elusive minimalism idealism".

By now, I had seven minutes to my call appointment.

In the rush of trying to make it on time, I decided figuring potential stains in the future would kill my exercise vibe. So emerald green it would be.

As soon as I turned around and made my way to the cashier, I heard the haunting voice of one of my friends, *"But Martha, is that what you really really want?"*

Immediately it struck me. I was making the easy choice. Though the striking, elegant green one is a colour I love and has the advantage of not getting easily stained, it was not the colour and mat that touched my soul at that moment.

Cleaning potential stains would be a struggle, which I can deal with by outsourcing a cleaner. Yes, my growth mindset in cleaning is minimal.

In summary, the pink mat was my true desire. In comparison, emerald green was a good enough alternative.

This encounter made me reflect on how often we accumulate good enough experiences and opportunities in our careers. We know that our ideal role, organisation, and compensation exist somewhere out there. Still, here we are, taking less and less.

In your compensation conversations, how often might you have used this phrase? "I will take what the company has to offer?"

And how often might you be underselling yourself by settling for a job that is 60% there while what you truly desire is at least a 90% match?

When might you have accepted compensation that is below what you know is your worth because you were afraid of never getting another opportunity?

Reflecting on this question will help you uncover moments when you've acted against your true desires. In most cases, what you really want is what feels like the more arduous path, but deep down also feels right.

Is the compensation you want a true reflection of the value you can create?

Get real buddy.

It's one thing to know what one wants; it's another to get others to buy into it. In this case, your future employer.

Is the compensation you are asking for what you truly believe you are worth? Do you have proof that you can replicate such value for the organisation you are seeking to join?

Now and then, I encounter job seekers asking for compensation that is way beyond the market rate. Yet, their results and way of selling themselves are way below expectations.

Furthermore, knowing your industry salary ranges is crucial in ensuring you are aligning your expectations accordingly. While some organisations might openly communicate their salary grades, in most cases, you will need to call upon your smart street skills (friends or past colleagues who know people and so on) into play. Research the ranges based on company brand, business goals and revenue targets, start-up vs established, local vs international, etc.

What are your financial goals for the next 2-3 years?

Besides thinking of the actual take-home salary you need to make right now, also think ahead.

Which part of your financial goals do you want to cover your salary from your day job?

What will these financial goals help you achieve? In other words, are you clear about what you are working towards in your life?

What are you willing to struggle for?

Without a list of your non-negotiables and the things you are willing to suffer for, negotiations will always feel hazy, confusing and out of your control.

When I chose to buy the pink yoga mat, I also decided to take responsibility for all the annoying stain removal ceremonies.

Conversations like the one below puzzle me.

Human: "I want to transition to a new industry."

Me: "And what is preventing you?"

Human: "The salary I am asking for is too high."

Me: "And what else?"

Person: "Perhaps, my skills and knowledge don't yet completely match what the organisations need in the roles I am seeking".

Me: "Hmmm. So what have you done so far to deal with these bottlenecks?"

Person: "I guess there is nothing I can do. I can't see myself taking a pay cut.

See the problem here?

What are the hidden benefits?

Often ask yourself, What 'hidden' benefits does this job opportunity offer me that my current one doesn't? We overlook this—a lot. Look beyond your take-home pay and those other fancy benefits they give you to buy your time, energy and expertise.

You are smarter than that. The real hidden benefits that will have the most impact on your career enhance your wellbeing as a human. And allow you to explore your potential fully.

Many of our other interests are not progressing because we take our negative work experiences and energy to our personal spaces. Hence we have no headspace to focus on driving our personal goals forward from our level best.

Map out everything the new job offers you. Including a better boss results in better mental health, which means you can focus on your work, deliver extraordinary results, and maximise your talents and curiosity. More flexible working hours or location saves you commute time and money, which means you can incorporate your other hobbies and interests into your days. With improved wellbeing, you have space and time to focus on your other side hustles and passion projects more deeply and with a clear mind!

Chapter 11

STOP LOOKING FOR A MEANINGFUL CAREER

Do you find meaningful work, or does it find you? Do you look for meaningful work, or do you create it? Can work, every day, be meaningful?

Disclaimer: Meaningful, fulfilling, satisfying, impactful, happy career, etc. Though we use different terms, we want the same thing. To feel our efforts and presence at work matters.

From seeking meaning to seeking successful experiences

Ok. The world has not been looking so good lately, and we want to do something about it.

Thanks to the gradually rising consciousness, more of us are persistently drawn into roles that connect us to something bigger than ourselves. Roles through which we can facilitate the creation of a better future. Since our careers have become our lives (sadly), we channel most of our longing for meaning or purpose into our work. And this is where the problems begin.

When our jobs or work environments frustrate us, we may lose our connection with our strengths, interests, worth, and confidence. Eventually, we conclude that our work lacks meaning. We are quick to jump (escape mode) to 'seeking something more meaningful'. We do this without paying much attention to 'what really matters to us' and 'why it uniquely matters to us'. We scan our circles for 'those pursuing meaningful work' and try to replicate their paths. Before we know it, we are back in the same rut we escaped from.

A common misconception that professionals in this phase proudly own is the single-mindedness that impactful or meaningful work can only manifest by transitioning into the development, social enterprise, or non-profit sector. In short, they are convinced that true fulfilment is found in jobs that 'try to save the world'.

While, to some extent, this thinking might hold some truth, there are dynamics that professionals have not considered. As a result, they set themselves up for discouragement. These dynamics include:1) There aren't enough jobs in these sectors for us all; hence the search can be lengthy, competitive, and time-consuming; 2) Often, professionals seeking such transitions lack clear, compelling reasons for the change, other than a desire to escape their current harsh realities. This results in less convincing pitches if not bitter ones; 3) Others lack the agility and adaptability needed to thrive in such workspaces; and, 4) The assumption that one's wealth of skills is automatically transferable and, thus, any organisation should be grateful for the abundance of expertise one brings. The latter never stops to halt me in my tracks.

For these reasons, it's essential to pause and look beyond our current triggers when the desire for an impactful career knocks on our doors. Doing so helps us uncover other factors that could have caused our lack of meaning. Consider setting up some time to reflect on the *real* reasons behind my desire for a meaningful career? What is beneath the reasons I believe I want this change?

Allowing these questions into our lives creates a space for us to explore tangibly what this sense of meaning looks like. The most obvious forms are: 'when we feel our strengths are creating value and we can see the impact of our work', or 'when our contribution is seen and recognised'. This gives us a sense of fulfilment that we can associate with 'my work is meaningful'. We experience a similar feeling when our role in shaping the organisation's strategy and vision is clear.

When the opposite occurs, for example, our work becomes mundane, does not seem to add value, or we fail to see the connection between our day-to-day tasks and the big picture of the organisation, we may feel purposeless. Worse, we may get trapped by comparing the state of our careers with that of professionals in our circles who, externally, seem to derive meaning from their work. Innocently, we forget that our perception may not be an accurate representation of our abilities or reality. When we do this, off goes our joy, and misery befalls our lives. Comparison is disastrous as it diverts our attention from creating a successful career life as defined by our own lenses.

You've probably met a few professionals whose work appears meaningless to your eyes, but they're ecstatic with it. In other cases, you must have crossed paths with professionals who work for 'dream employers', an organisation that's changing the world, yet they walk around feeling incomplete. Or perhaps you overheard a coworker rant about their work, which, in your opinion, is more than perfect?

Why does this happen? Individually, we use different meters to gauge what meaningful work is to us and, consequently, what it means to succeed in our careers. When the meter falls short of our expectations, we feel disconnected and unsatisfied.

When you uncover the layers of your search for meaning, you will find the underlying reason: so you can feel successful. We want to arrive at a place where we are pursuing work that allows us to spend our time, energy and effort contributing in invaluable ways. And, as a result, we achieve our most profound personal desires or preconceived outcomes. This sense of tangible accomplishment closely connects to what meaningful work looks or feels like for us.

Is it possible, then, that if one was to strive for clarity (getting honest about what matters to them) and owning (the harder path) what success authentically means for them, and then commit themselves to pursue only those job opportunities and organisations aligned with this criteria, they could get closer to feeling more fulfilled?

It's not guaranteed. But it's an idea worth a try.

Let's explore a framework that can help you discover what a meaningful career uniquely looks and feels like for you. The cumulative sum of these meaningful experiences is your measure of career success.

Mondays: Magic vs Mundane

It's Monday morning. Work is calling! How will you feel when you truly love, are content and connected with what you do?

Check-in with yourself:

- What is everything that needs to be in place for every day of my work to be magic-filled? Challenge yourself to write at least 50 things. It's surprising what your subconscious might reveal!
- What type of work tasks, if pursued every day or for at least 70% of my time, would make my life more pleasurable?
- Which are my non-negotiable values for me to thrive in the workplace? Why do these matter to me?

Your Investment vs Returns

How will you know that the time, energy and talent you are investing in an organisation is worthwhile?

Check-in with yourself:

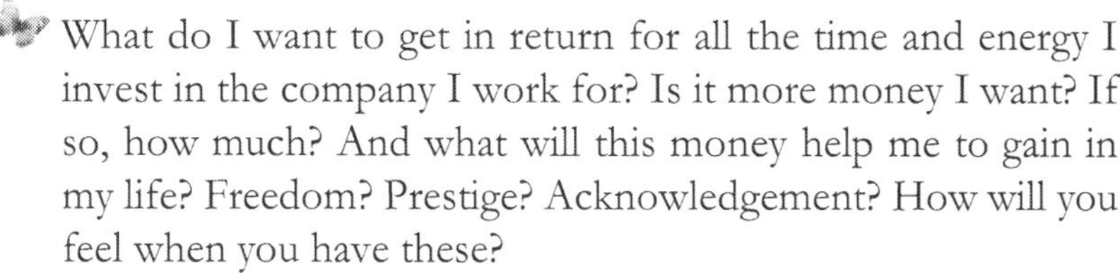

- What do I want to get in return for all the time and energy I invest in the company I work for? Is it more money I want? If so, how much? And what will this money help me to gain in my life? Freedom? Prestige? Acknowledgement? How will you feel when you have these?
- Or perhaps it's your well being preserved and protected. If so, how does this look and feel in tangible form? A month or two off every year? More family time? An organisation that offers mental health support? Bosses and workmates, who create a safe space for you to thrive and express what you need freely? Work from anywhere option? Total autonomy over the working schedule? What does a career that supports your wellbeing mean for you?

Your highest aspirations vs impact

- To feel successful in your career, what is the balance needed between your highest career aspirations and the impact you are creating? For example, imagine being a top leader of a global energy company that is not concerned with sustainable environmental practices. Would you still feel successful?
- How will it feel when your highest aspirations and the impact you are creating positively align?

Conduct this exercise every six months or so to keep yourself in check if the needs that matter the most are still being met. This way, you decrease the chances of being caught by the surprise of 'how did things get so bad in my career' several years down the line. Yet, it will be no surprise as the clues were there all along the way.

Pro tip 1: If you feel incomplete or unsatisfied in other areas of your life, resist the urge to get lost in your work to fill in the gaps. This is another risky route that will only make you feel more resentful when your work fails to meet your expectations. Instead, seek the help you need to uplift and reinvent your life to achieve fulfilment in the other areas of your life. Prioritise doing what you must to create more peace, self-acceptance and abundance in your life and then resume figuring out your career hurdles.

Pro tip 2: I have yet to meet a human who has not sought recognition, support, validation, and connection, at least once in their career lifetime, from their colleagues and bosses. Initially, it's all about work. With time, sadly and unknowingly, it is to affirm their identity and self-worth. When this backfires, our self-esteem crashes, and we are devastated. At this point, it's easy to think one lacks purpose, meaning, or something is incomplete in their life. This is unfair to our glorious selves. We need to constantly remind ourselves that, in the world of work, nobody owes us anything. And the truth is, with or without our work, we are already whole.

From finding to creating meaning, every damn day!

We now know that:

- Not all of us will be lucky enough to find world-changing jobs.
- No organisation is perfect.
- Without self-determined measures of career success, one is tempted to compare themselves using the wrong lenses.
- Looking for the ultimate sense of completion in our work sets us up for disappointment.

How do we move ahead in navigating our need for meaning and purpose that we will continue to seek to fulfil through our work?

We begin by recognising and avoiding these traps:

- Waiting *to* find a meaningful job one day.
- Waiting for our employers to create meaningful roles for us.
- Complaining about how our work has no meaning while doing nothing about it.
- Settling on the lie, 'this is how work is'.

And instead, shift to a more proactive approach by creating windows of opportunity to experience meaning and purpose every day. Commit to asking yourself frequently, "What tiny actions can I take today for my work to feel more purposeful?" Trust me; there is always something you can do.

A good place to start is by taking advantage of the resources that our bodies are. Simply put, we learn to tap into our happiness hormones more. Completing tasks, and celebrating our low hanging fruits, triggers our dopamine hormone, making us feel good. We feel good because we have stretched ourselves to accomplish something. I have no doubt you'd love to feel good about creating tangible results every day. No matter how tedious or annoying the task might be, you deserve applause for seeing it to completion. So go on and give it to yourself.

In addition, create slots of 2-3 minute breaks after every task. This is your sacred acknowledgement time.

Whether it's clear to you how the task matters to the big picture or not, you accomplished it. Recognising yourself in this way relieves the pressure of unrequited approval.

There is a caveat, though. To truly enjoy the rush of these sacred acknowledgement breaks, you must have chosen to approach your tasks purposefully from the beginning. Often, we rush through our to-do lists to get to the next one. As a result, we miss the opportunity and joy to acknowledge ourselves at their completion.

Finally, try incorporating meaningful interactions and approaches into your daily work tasks and interactions with various stakeholders. This is where the little things challenge comes into play.

The little things challenge

In the end, it's the little things that become big things.

Experiment with bringing little meaning into your everyday work for the next 30 days.

Every morning, ask yourself, "In what small way can I create purpose, meaning, or whatever makes me feel good about the tasks and experiences I face today?"

Here are a few ideas...

With your team

In every interaction, decide that you will show up and contribute at least one little thing.

Choose to surprise one person with a positive gesture every two weeks.

Block 30 minutes to support a junior employee who you've seen struggle in a particular area that is your superpower.

Listen to a colleague for a minute longer.

Stop by a colleague's workstation and acknowledge one thing you admire about their traits.

Over the coffee break, recognise a team member who has been putting in extra hours to see a project through.

To your customers or clients

Before getting too serious about business, take the first five minutes to genuinely inquire about how other aspects of their lives are progressing. What excites them today? What good things are happening? You will be shocked to learn that they haven't paused to think of this last one in a long time. And what a blessing it is that you have asked me.

In your client meetings, lead by simply asking, "How can I support you today?" And let them speak about what's alive in them for five minutes. Work with whatever comes up.

Consider sending personalised and thoughtful messages to your customers or business partners on special events in their lives. Let them know you appreciate working together.

Create meaning in your day-to-day work tasks.

This may be new, so begin by auditing yourself:

How do I approach my tiniest tasks? Mindlessly? Or with great intention and a focus on only creating masterpieces?

When I work, how often do I fully use my attention, energy and talents to create exemplary results?

When was the last time I connected with my manager for a chat to clarify how my work relates to the organisation's strategy and goals?

How often do I take time to clarify the purpose of my tasks before moving into action?

The intention behind your actions is the mother of purpose.

So you still want work that saves the world?

Fine.

I get it. You strongly believe that you will experience the highest fulfilment in your career if you invest your talents and energy in work that directly impacts the lives of the people and the society you live in.

You want to contribute to causes such as ending poverty, saving the planet, gender equality, quality education, clean water provision, clean energy, and the like through your career.

Perhaps you find yourself caught up in non-ending reflections and contemplations about what social causes you care most about. Does it matter which path you choose? I tend to think not. If you have a list of two to three areas that irritate you about the state of the world and are confident you'll devote your life to finding solutions in these areas, then, by all means, roll the dice and start anywhere. The world has too many issues to resolve. No matter where you start, you are guaranteed to move the needle.

For recruiters, it is a pity to encounter highly qualified professionals unable to articulate a compelling 'why' behind their transition. Others have barely bothered to dip a finger to test the waters of the areas they passionately want to shift to.

Transitioning into the development work world is much more efficient and productive when one carefully crafts and diligently follows through with their career experiments (refer to the Experiments chapter).

The more experiments you run, the faster you determine what problems ignite your fire and the type of roles that bring your magic to life. Furthermore, this gives you hands-on experience of how it will feel to work in such environments. As you encounter and resolve real challenges, you gather valuable information and insights. These will, in the future, guide you to make a conscious decision if this is the right path for you.

Such experiences over time will elevate your candidacy. Positioning you as an action-oriented solution creator, which is what the development world truly needs.

Chapter 12

YOUR CAREER BUSINESS

In case you haven't already, drop the idea that you are 'just an employee. This is a trap that keeps you safely indulging in smallness.

You are the owner of talents, skills, and knowledge that organisations need to thrive. Your mission is to create compelling value for organisations. And you are highly rewarded for your investment.

You've chosen and are committed to being the driver of your career. And you constantly reinvent your expertise so you can keep your competitive edge alive.

Become a badass CEO of your career

I can't overemphasise this. Every organisation must find the fastest route to justify its existence, realise its vision, and create the desired impact. Whether that's maximising its profits, increasing its market share, return on investment, or changing the world, any organisation's existence is irrelevant without achieving its bottom line. It's thus only fair that those whose efforts and services can support the acceleration of attaining an organisation's goals should tag along. For professionals, the clearer one's vision and goals are, the faster it is for one to connect with organisations aligned to their career aspirations.

Organisations need you to achieve their bottom line. You, on the other hand, thanks to capitalism, need a source of livelihood, and you've chosen employment as that source. Hence both parties play essential roles in enabling each other to achieve their respective goals. The playground, however, doesn't always feel or look fair. Many professionals are playing the 'I need you more' game while many employers play the 'without me you can't make it' game. Consequently destabilising the value creation chain.

No wonder many professionals hop around so much, hoping to bump into organisations that might see and appreciate their value. While at the same time trying to prove to past employers (mostly the bad ones) they can make it without them. Sometimes, one is lucky to find a home that allows one to unleash their talents and potential. Other times one might run out of choices and is unfortunately forced to eat the humble pie. This attitude is a silent killer to our greatness and an enhancer for inflated organisations' egoism. Employers, on the other hand, are convinced of the 'talent scarcity myth'. Since this book is about working professions, we will let employers figure out their part for now.

As your career progresses, taking the driver's seat is not an accessory but a prerequisite for your success. It would be best if you quickly dropped the 'I need them more' mindset and move into the 'I am a value creator' mindset. Initially, when you begin playing with this idea, you might realise you do not feel like an equal player. This is normal as you are not used to seeing yourself this way.

When you play like a value creator, you know, own, and compellingly articulate your worth. You take every role as an opportunity to step into your space boldly. You approach your tasks purposefully and meticulously. You own your work goals and pursue to deliver nothing short of exceptional work. You proactively keep yourself informed and engaged in the latest business and industry trends. Not because it's in your job description to do so, but because you know this is what you must do to stay ahead of the game.

Your forward-thinking nature positions you as a creative problem solver. You are resourceful and enthusiastic in supporting the organisation to achieve its goals. In every business conversation, you show up as a solution creator instead of a bringer of challenges.

You recognise that organisations' central pain point in volatile economies is how to keep evolving to meet the constantly changing demands of their customers. Accordingly, you remain relevant by accelerating your ability to master new skills and knowledge. You immerse yourself in diverse and disruptive experiences to sharpen your agility skills.

To master this new way of being in your career, you need to empathise with the ways of successful and competitive businesses.

Step into their shoes and perceive your career as a vision-driven goal-oriented business. Create a compelling value proposition and competitive strategy for achieving your goals.

When you think and show up this way, you level up in demanding employers what you want, without blinking, as you are super confident of what you are capable of.

So how do we get you to this desired state? Below, I am sharing a comprehensive list of questions that will help you reevaluate your self-perception concerning employment. Call yourself for a board meeting and painstakingly respond to each of these. They will challenge you. You will feel a little or lots of discomfort. If you hang around with these questions long enough, you will begin to experience a shift in how you perceive your worth. Your approaches to positioning yourself will dramatically change. Ultimately you will notice your level of confidence begins to rise.

To exhaust this exercise, you will need a couple of paced hours to get through each section. This, however, is not a one time exercise. You will need to revisit these quarterly or sooner to keep track of how you are evolving.

Your Vision

What is the vision of your career business? You know, the most significant impact you want to create? The trends you want to shape and the legacy you will leave behind?

____

____

What value is this business creating for the world? To the organisations you serve?

____

____

What 2-3 scary and exciting goals do you need to start pursuing for the next ten years to get a few steps closer to this vision?

____

____

Your strategies

What innovative strategies are you pursuing to lead you to your scary & exciting goals?

____

____

What initiatives are you partaking in to ensure your career business stays agile and future-ready in a highly competitive market?

What processes do you need to optimise so your career business can run efficiently and effectively?

In what ways is this career business investing its energy, time and money in unproductive ways?

What is the support system you need for learning, sharing, and exchanging ideas? Have you hired a mentor, a coach, or another thought leader in your field to guide you?

Your brand

What is the total value you've created in your career business journey so far? Do you have a track record that proves what you are capable of?

How is your brand visibility and perception in the market? Are you seen where you must be seen for your work to be recognised? What channels are you capitalising on to enhance these?

How are you constantly reinventing yourself, so you remain on top of your professional game in a fast-changing world?

Who are your ambassadors or salespeople who know your brand so well and honestly believe in your ability to deliver value?

How do you stay on the lookout for unique opportunities that match your talents and interests?

What opportunities, ideas, seem too out of the box, and you know these are the ones you need to pursue aggressively to elevate your brand?

Is how you pitch yourself compelling? Is it a 100% reflection of the value you can create for your customers (in this case, potential employers)?

Your rewards and performance

What underperforming aspects of your career business are you tolerating? What are you protecting by doing so?

____

____

What aspects of your career are performing exemplary well and need more acknowledgement?

____

____

Who are the people in your team (friends, colleagues, acquaintances) that your career business has outgrown and are thus lagging your goals behind? How will you let them go?

____

____

How do you recognise, reward and celebrate your achievements?

____

____

Would you hire yourself?

Now imagine you are the CEO of a leading company in your industry. Pick a name right at this moment. A company that inspires and challenges you. Perhaps one you've secretly dreamt of working for.

Then review each of your responses to the questions above. And then ask yourself: Would you hire yourself?

____

____

Chapter 13

YOUR SPARK WILL SET YOU FREE

You can be free

Free from the masks, the hiding, the suppressing of the supernova being you are

Free to show up in your magnificent self

You can be free

Free to finally express those obstinate longings in your heart.

Free to chase what secretly thrills you

You can be free

Free to let the world experience your spark

Free to be you

Our spark is our truth

We all have one.

That twinkle in our eyes when everything aligns.

That beat in our hearts that longs to dance.

That call screaming quietly for our attention to bring it to life.

That unrevealed dream that haunts our waking hours.

That idea, whose mention, suddenly removes the years from our faces.

That interest pulling us strongly into the unknown.

That fire that burns in our bellies. Consuming our darkest nights.

That stubborn sound of silence whispering: "You can do it".

That force that drives us to the edge of insanity to give only our very best.

That gut feeling, so indescribable that only in silence can you put it into words.

That thing we want to do, and it is what we must do. Because nothing else makes us feel this alive.

Our spark is how we want to show up in the world. It's us raw and real, with no embellishments. It's how we want to create, contribute and shape the world around us if we had no limitations. Our spark is in our refusal to play it safe. It's those traits that others miss when we leave the room. It's those things that a stranger admires about us and remarks that just by being us, we changed their world. We wonder what we did. We did nothing. We were simply living in our most natural state.

Our spark is in those moments when we want to shout from the top of our lungs, "Yes, I love that! I'd like to have more of that in my life".

Even when we try to disguise it, the mystery in our eyes sells us out. Or that almost unnoticed extra curve on our lips when we smile at something that makes us happy, but we are afraid of being seen smiling. For such a smile would give away our vulnerability. How could allowing our light to shine betray us? Isn't concealing our truth the ultimate betrayal?

Our spark is sometimes disguised in those obvious little things our bosses really pay us for but don't exactly tell us so. Yet, they will do anything from the extremes of fake kindness to manipulation for us to hang around.

It's a force dressed in curiosity, interests, things that frustrate us or those that haunt us as we go about our mundane days.

Other times, our spark might trigger a sense of healthy envy when we see others living in a way we admire and yearn for ourselves.

It's when we let down our guard that our spark flows through us. We glow, our eyes smile, our hearts sing, our minds buzz, and our feet won't stay still. In such moments, we are confident about one thing. This is what we were born for!

Take a moment and reconnect with your truth; what makes you feel this way? What is your spark? When you allow yourself to bask in your spark, you are more joyful and excited about your life and work.

Mine is limitless enthusiasm and a deep, addictive longing to experience the beauty of life in its grandest and purest form every damn day. It's in my immersion and communion with nature, the mystical, and all things artistically magnificent. It's an endless hunger to create. A desire so strong, I can't do anything else but create. It's an unshakable faith in the infinite seeds of possibilities that lie within each human soul.

My spark comes alive through writing, photography, imaginative work, creating new programs, leading in crisis, solving problems, dreaming up big ideas that could change the world, and when I curate or host safe and transformational spaces for human connection and learning. These are the various vessels through which I channel and share my spark with the world. When you are clear about what your spark is, your career options expand.

I was on a hike recently when someone made this peculiar comment, "One day, I would love to see the world through Martha's eyes. "To see what she sees through her camera that I don't see through mine," she says. When your spark is lit, everyone can see it. Everyone is drawn to it. You inspire others to seek what theirs could be.

To allow your spark to shine is a risk you take. Others might rebel against it. Take no offence. They lack the bravery to stand in their sunshine.

Connecting and owning your spark is another of those magic ingredients for success in your career. You might still succeed either way, but you are way better off if your spark is your guiding light. When you are confident in what makes you come alive, you are empowered to boldly approach your work and new opportunities. The difference between those in the driver's seat of their careers and those hanging out in the back seat is that the former choose to do everything possible to light, fan, and preserve their spark. They know this is the secret that makes their career adventures worthy. It helps them navigate the hurdles and keeps them warm when the journey gets cold.

What activities, conversations, tasks, experiences bring you joy and boost your eagerness to take action? That's an excellent place to start looking for clues if you feel far from knowing what your spark is.

Authenticity is Efficiency

Your spark is your most authentic self, naked. It's when you've stripped off your fears and lay yourself bare, revealing only that which screams: "Hey! This is who I beautifully am. This is who I want you to let be". No, scratch that. "This is who I'm allowing myself to be."

No wonder we hide it safely. In a world that advocates "how to be to fit in" rather than "how to be yourself," this level of exposing ourselves is unfamiliar and, in most cases, unacceptable.

Unfortunately, all these cover-ups and hiding games cost us time, joy, and our potential. It is highly inefficient to spend our limited life years in this manner.

I met one of my clients in the mall the other day.

I was wearing my signature red braids pinned up in my very best version of ruggedness. Like most days, I was hurriedly making my way to an important meeting. She looked at me and said: "Your hairstyle looks amazing! How do you manage to make this whole red hair thing authentically yours like that?"

To be honest, I was a little surprised, mainly because, of all days, this was the one I had left the house in the most haste.

She went on to ask how often I visited the salon to style my hair.

I don't. I throw it up and tie it with any hair band within my visibility. Move a few braids around, and I am ready to move. Brief and efficient. Then, I step out and work it.

Working it. That is the other thing about bringing your spark to life. Working your spark fans it.

"I guess when you fully step into your raw authenticity, everything flows naturally and easily," was the immediate response that made sense and felt true.

As I mentioned earlier in the experiments chapter, my path of career alignment led me to leave behind two jobs. At one of my farewell parties, my boss shared this candid and mind-blowing feedback with the team.

"You know, when Martha showed up in my office for that final interview, I was shocked by how bright and lively her eyes were. Who was this human so full of life and enthusiasm? At that moment, it immediately hit me. This is exactly what we needed in the organisation and, specifically, in this department—an energised individual who would channel fresh perspectives into ongoing, highly demanding, and ambitious projects. And so I hired her."

Interestingly, I had never worked in a similar setup or had the direct skills and knowledge needed for the job. At the end of the day, it's my enthusiasm, sparkling eyes, out-of-the-box fresh perspectives and a solid ability to dive into the unknown and figure things out that got the job done.

By keeping my true self alive at the interviews, I helped the hiring team gain more clarity on what the department needed to achieve its goals.

Yet, this is no special case. Throughout my recruiting career, I've encountered many instances where organisations gain clarity about the essence of the role, how it fits into the existing team, and the unique value that a new hire can bring, during the ongoing hiring conversations. No matter how much effort is put into crafting super clear job descriptions (which only a handful of companies do anyway), meeting potential candidates always inspires a new way of thinking about the potential of the role. All the insights gained are fed back into the ongoing recruiting process to ensure that the final hire is their best bet.

While organisations will stress recruiters like mad, no employer expects to find a perfect candidate. But they ask us to find superheroes anyway. In my experience, when a candidate is too good to be true, the hiring team is often worried if there is something (negative) they are missing. Not to mention the dozens of times we get bitten for hiring a good-looking profile who fails to execute at the expected level of standards.

My point in all this? Stop hiding those traits, desires, secret dreams, and superpowers you possess. The world needs your unique self. Stop assuming you know for sure what employers want. In most cases, they may think they do. Until you walk into the room and realise they haven't fully assessed and internalised the role requirements against the organisation's actual needs. Or, in your natural state, you say something that sparks a new way of thinking about the purpose the role could play in driving the organisation's goals forward. If you end up not being hired because you let your authenticity shine, consider it your salvation from misalignment. Nothing wastes your time and leads to unnecessary frustration in your career, like being in the wrong role or organisation. Consider that your authenticity saved the day for you and the organisation.

Mastering Self Reinvention

The legendary Chinese Philosopher Lao Tzu once said, "When I let go of what I am, I become what I might be."

Let's be honest; you can barely keep up with the changes happening in the world right now. So why hang onto the idea of who you've been all this time when there are chances you could be so much more?

Entertain the idea that your spark could become a wildfire. Step out of mediocrity and safety nets. Break yourself free from the traps that deny your light from shining. Start playing at the level of your highest aspirations and potential. Believe with all you've got that your spark can transform organisations. And then go out there and create change.

As you advance in your career, you will naturally seek to become the best at what you do. Focus your efforts on becoming the best at the things that light up your world. Fan your spark into an ongoing fire that propels you to go full force after your goals.

You *could* wake up one day as a brand new person. Recognise that continuing to hide in the shadows of your greatness costs you too much. Put on new energy, new positive vibes, new magical thoughts, new life-enhancing beliefs, and attitude because *you decided to.* You understand that this type of change is complex, but it is the difficulty that serves your progress.

You can surprise the world by how much you've evolved in what seems like an overnight shift. Let your social circles barely remember who you were last week, last month.

Decide right now that you will put on new lenses every morning—lenses to perceive yourself and your career powerfully. Like the supernova you are.

Like night and day, change how you talk about your abilities. Bring more power and boldness to how you describe your achievements. Own your successes, big and small.

Adopt new healthy habits for your mind, soul, and body, so you are super energised to go after what you truly desire. You know your wellbeing is the fuel for high productivity and exemplary performance. Hence, you don't compromise.

Become a master at letting go of your BS. All that shitty stuff you've believed about yourself. All the doubts and fears about what you can and can not do, stick them all in a big trash bag and throw it into a moving garbage truck.

Once you taste the joy and freedom that resides on the other side of your self-created BS, you will never want to go back there.

Then embrace your gifts and talents. Get so good at your craft that everyone who interacts with your work is astonished by how you remarkably deliver excellent and impactful results, so effortlessly, every single time.

Filter ruthlessly over the years until all that is left on your tasks list are the things you truly enjoy.

Decide from now on that you will belong to new circles of influence. Connect deeply with people who understand where you are and where you want to go. If you have, and you probably have, outgrown your circles but are too afraid to jump, jump anyway. Your new tribe is out there, desperately waiting for you.

Oh, you wonder where all the courage to do all these things will come from? Worry not; all you need is to put your first foot forward, and the next, and then the next. I am pretty confident that you can manage that. Look back at the millions of tiny steps you've taken so far! Just one step forward at a time. Before you know it, you've crawled yourself halfway there. Now you have the bravery to move faster.

Learn new skills and bodies of knowledge. Confuse people with your ability to move flawlessly in diverse conversations. Talk about business, science, technology, philosophy, art, politics and everything that positions you as a sundry exciting human.

Pick a new area and become a maestro. Shock yourself by studying everything you've ever been curious about in just six months. You know you can. If only you could reduce the amount of time, you spend on meaningless tasks that divert your attention away from your true desires.

Change how you speak - be strong, firm in your tone of voice, go deep in your conversations, learn new vocabulary. "I'm fine," and "It's all good" are overused, boring, and a spark killer. Say, instead, that you are fantastically engaged in your life and are super excited about the amazing things you are pursuing. Say your life rocks; you are grateful for all the incredible events unfolding.

Speak your mind often, but express only what truly matters. Otherwise, listen. Listen so deeply to yourself and others so you can discover more gems and sparks hidden in you. The ones often revealed in silence.

Become that person you know you should be and you want to be. Commit to yourself right now that when your past boss or colleagues meet you a year from now, they will be astounded by the magnificent transformation you've undergone.

Imagine them hardly recognising you, passing you by the street and turning back to confirm why you look so familiar. You are free to smile and politely respond: "Sure, I have that familiar face".

See yourself as that goal smasher, ass-kicker, authentic human that you know, deep down, you are. Then work towards becoming them.

Do it silently. Do it stubbornly. Do it scared anyway.

Create an alter ego if you must. I embodied two goddesses while writing this book: Diana, the Roman goddess, for her fighting spirit and her hunt into the wild. And Seshat, an Egyptian goddess of wisdom, writing, and knowledge. These two guardian angels showered me with the fierceness I needed to channel this book. They enabled me to unleash the wailing hero within me.

Your alter ego is your other, super incredible self, begging to be let out. It is your faithful ally who wants to help you on your path to achieving greatness. You know all those people you admire? You are attracted to them because your inner hero sees themselves in them. Start challenging yourself to do everything your hero would do. While at it, bring some humour and lightness to it.

Let taking yourself less and less seriously be the magic ingredient of your reinvention.

Once, I was trekking in the Himalayas in India. Thanks to avalanches and unpredictable weather, our summit was cut short. I had two choices: to descend with my group through the same route we had ascended or join two strangers on an adventure to search for hot water springs.

There are many things I am capable of, but descending into a foreign and dangerous terrain with two people I barely know is not one of them. So, on the night of decision-making, I summoned the alter ego of a former acquaintance who would have no qualms about taking such a risk. How would she experience such a journey? How would she think? What precautions would she take? This is one of the risky travel decisions I have made that was surprisingly rewarding. These strangers turned out to be beautiful, kind, and free-spirited souls.

Still on the edge of making bold changes? Remember, you owe no one but yourself an explanation of why you sound, look or show up differently. You do you. Because it's fun. There is nothing you want more than to see your hopes finally breathe. You love seeing yourself become everything you could never imagine. You love to reinvent yourself because you know your light looks good on you.

You know that lighting your spark sets you free.

And freedom accelerates your growth.

Drop the Idea that You can Be Great at Everything

The idea that you can be great at everything is faulty. It gets in the way of your spark coming to life. Mastery is achieved through focus and ruthless filtering. Enduring through roles and work activities that divert most of your attention and energy from your spark is, needless to say, a waste of your time and restricted by the limitless potential paradox.

If you want to maximise how you utilise your spark to create an epic career, choose wisely what you will focus on. As the artist, you are, focus on refining your craft over time. Can you outshine everyone in your profession? Give it some years of hardcore dedication and watch yourself rise.

Perhaps you are doubtful. I challenge you to look around and spot the most successful individuals you know. Pick any field or industry. From sports to agriculture. Study carefully the professionals who are moving the goalposts, achieving incredible results, creating massive change, and leaving a legacy in their fields. What are the chances that they are great at everything?

When you devote most of your time, energy, and spark to work that is aligned with your spark, you will quickly light up your career. Remember to build a support army for all other tasks that steal your time and drain your energy. Be careful, though, that your support system doesn't create another chain of energy and time-sucking cycles. Thus, delegate tactfully, only to other masters.

While on your journey of accelerating, advancing, or transitioning, accepting offers for jobs that comprise a significant amount (70% +) of tasks that drain your energy, leaving you feeling frustrated, is an automatic setup for failure and a slow death trap for your spark.

Perhaps your employer wants you to be all-rounded. You nod your head and remind them of how much value you are creating through your areas of mastery.

Telling yourself that you have been through worse and can hack roles or workplaces that suck the life out of you is unkind to your spark. It is the type of fault-positive enthusiasm that will send you to an early career grave—exhausted and lifeless.

You don't want that. You want to be free. Free to be. Free to create and contribute powerfully. So go, find and fan your spark. Step into your true powerful self and watch how your world of work transforms. Do yourself right.

Chapter 14

WANT TO ACCELERATE? FUCK THE SYSTEM!

The learning approaches that have shaped your career so far are outdated. To get to the next level, you must be willing to learn and grow unorthodoxically.

The system or your potential?

You possess immense abilities. If intentionally developed and strategically deployed, these could create meaningful value for the organisations you work for and bring you enormous satisfaction in your career.

The first thing you are most likely to think of when considering a career overhaul, promotion or change, is up-skill. Which is why you will translate this to mean enrolling in a formal learning institution. You're probably thinking about it right now. Hold that thought until the end of the chapter, and if by then you still feel it's the right path for you, then, by all means possible, go ahead!

Over the years, serendipity and I have formed such a strong bond that she never fails to show up when I need her most. For instance, I scratched my empty head cluelessly, wondering what this chapter was all about; I recalled a fascinating encounter that reminded me of my love-hate relationship with systems. Social, political, taxation, work processes, family, education, etc. All systems, really.

Some guy in my apartment building: Martha, can I ask you a question?

Me: Yes, sure.

Some guy: You shouldn't put that chair there.

Me to myself: *Boy, that's no question. It sounds more like an order.*

Me: Oh really, why so?

Some guy: Because everyone else will start putting their stuff there.

Me to myself: And why precisely is that my problem?

Me: I have one parking spot. Can we assume that is the space the chair is occupying?

Some guy: But that's not a car.

Me: But is that my parking spot?

Before my nerves could run wild, it occurred to me that this conversation reminded me so much of our education system. You follow the instructions. You learn what is prescribed. Whether you like it or not, often you have to follow rules that you know very well don't matter in the grand scheme of things. Thinking differently barely matters. Your role is to fit into how things are done and question Nothing. Sometimes you are given a little room for your creativity to come alive, but not too much of it to rock the boat.

Thanks to our very theory-heavy minus real-life-stuff education approach, you acquire just enough information to barely scratch the surface of your potential. Sadly, many organisation leaders have also copy-pasted a similar approach in their workplaces, accelerating the weight and impact of 'the system' in our lives. Any ideas or opinions that seem too out of the norm, too provocative, too elevating - that stuff is shunned.

While it's easy to blame these institutions, the real issue arises when we fail to challenge and update the systems in place in response to our changing needs. As a result, we have become the servants of the past.

It's unfortunate that we rarely create systems that enable us to tap our limitless potential, fully utilise our capabilities, explore our interests, and help us self-actualise. Once you grasp this, your approach to evolving and growing your career takes a sharp turnaround. You have no other alternative but to recreate your learning and development system.

I once went through a phase of interviews with top global MBA schools. Now, I have no objections to pursuing masters degrees and all. Back then, I foolishly thought it was my gate pass to the next level of my potential. The reality is, I was running away from putting my ideas and presence to the world and fully stepping into my power.

With close to 15 years of interviewing (...and boy! I have interviewed all sorts of creatures. From 5-year-olds, potential presidents, top-notch founders, social intra and entrepreneurs, and C-Suite business leaders globally). I can boldly say I know many things when it comes to being bullshitted in an interview. Candidates do it. Interviewers do it. We are all bullshitting our way to what we want. Please don't tell me you haven't done it even once? Then perhaps there is Nothing you want that badly?

Back to the MBA interviews. It made sense that I found the interview questions underwhelming: too scripted, uninterested in the human, and many sent me to the death bed of boredom. You know that moment when you are going all the way, positioning yourself as a unique individual because you are anyway. So you throw a gem about how amazing you are, only to be hit by an unrelated follow-up question. And zero acknowledgement or curiosity to learn more about what you have just shared. A fake smile accompanied by a nod that tells you: your interviewer thinks you are an alien! Sigh. Such an anticlimax.

Though I have to confess, I have always been a rebellious student when it comes to learning systems. I remember not caring about my low Kikuyu - my tribal language subject - in second and third grades. Now, there are about 68 tribal languages in Kenya. Kikuyu is one. We also have a national language, Swahili, and English as the business language. Back then, for the first 3-4 years of one's education, knowledge was disseminated in one's first language, often the local tribal language. Since then, with urbanisation, intermarriages and a little change in the education system, things have evolved.

I, however, was a unique case as my tribal language was not my first language. I grew up in a multicultural environment on the coast, and my first language was Swahili. As the universe would have it, we moved back to my rural home at some point. And that led to me joining a local school, where Kikuyu was the instructional language.

Besides being taught in Kikuyu, we also had to learn the language itself. Everyone laughed at my accent. My grades were very much below average. Fact wise, though, it made no sense to struggle to comprehend a subject that would soon become irrelevant. I decided it was easier to manipulate the system by performing better in other subjects while waiting to be transferred to a fully English-speaking school.

This defiance followed me passionately to high school. I sucked at Physics and Maths. Who feels like me right now? In grade 11, frustrated by all the concepts and the lack of customised guidance, I chose to wing it with these two subjects. I barely touched these two for the next year, which resulted in below-average final year results, but because I focused on my strong subjects, I achieved an overall grade of A-.

Then there were the wonderful years of university. Let's just say I am pretty sure some classmates didn't like me that much, which is no surprise when you dare to be different. You see, I was the girl who held the class hostage for as long as it took if a concept a lecturer was sharing did not make sense.

I honestly can't tell from where this stubbornness germinated. Still, I know it's been my guide in staying true to my strengths and talents while disregarding everything that doesn't serve my growth.

And you, too, should care about where you focus your money, time and energy when it comes to accelerating your learning and growth. The secret is to find that sweet spot between your gifts and interests and what organisations truly care about.

Employers care about two things

Over the last 12 years, my consulting encounters with hundreds of growth-oriented organisations has majorly focused on creating talent strategies to accelerate their goals. These experiences have narrowed my understanding of what employers deeply care about.

Let's explore how these influence how you go about your learning and development journeys.

> *Can you do the job exceptionally well?*
>
> And,
>
> *How quickly can you adapt and remain agile as the company evolves to meet the needs of a fast-changing world?*

How you demonstrate your competence and confidence in the above two questions is key to unlocking the opportunities you are seeking. This requires one to be strategic and efficient in growing exponentially the diverse skills and mindsets that organisations need.

How do you learn to do a job exceptionally well? By approaching your work with strong dedication, meticulous execution, and mastering the essential aspects of the work that create the most value. On the other hand, agility and adaptability are life skills and mindsets acquired from various experiences, including adjusting your life effectively in the face of a global pandemic or exposing yourself to new challenges or adventures.

If these are the two key areas organisations deeply care about. What does this mean for your learning and development journey? Is signing up for another traditional schooling approach your first path? Perhaps only when you are 100% sure it is the only path.

And how do you get this 100% clarity that this is your best move?

Again, through action. Experiment with the ideas shared in this chapter and see where they lead you. Believe me, when I say that I care about your money, the unnecessary headaches, lost time with family and friends, abandoned creative and volunteering projects, forsaken hobbies, burnout, and all that baggage that comes with further education while life happens.

For many of us, I understand the conditioning that skills and knowledge are acquired through going to formal institutions is ocean deep. If you belong to this club, I am sending you energetic hugs right now.

I, too, have fallen into this trap several times. For example, this time, I decided to upgrade my coaching skills. The natural thing to do was enrol in a formal institution. Coincidentally, at the same time, I met a fantastic friend who is also a thought-leader in the coaching space. We immediately clicked. She guided me in determining the best school for me.

One day, long after I had settled on a good enough program, I shared how this new learning experience was building on what I'd been experimenting. I had quickly realised I already possessed many of the skills and knowledge that were being taught. It felt strange to receive structure and language for something I already knew instinctively.

She nodded, smiled, and confidently responded, "You know what Martha, some of us are naturals".

If technology can do it better than you, forget it

Not so long ago, there was a time when no one could imagine a human surgical operation performed by a doctor and completed in less than 6 hours. Today, a cesarean section procedure takes under 60 minutes. After hundreds of experiments, we now have many non-invasive surgeries popping up all over the place. Some super confident peeps in the world of health and innovation argue that robots have a high potential to replace doctors by 2035. Obviously, not all doctors will go home. All this is subject to several years of more iterations. However, you must agree, the audacity to even think this way is remarkable.

Chances are, you will probably be alive to see the first 100% robotic surgery. If you think this is obvious, as the healthcare industry needs this innovation to enhance efficiency, effectiveness, accessibility, and save more lives, then wait until you discover experiments on creating 100% robotic live bands. Not to mention all those biohacking games to extend human life!

None of us will escape the innovation and technology craze set to take over specific industries and jobs. It is your responsibility to stay on top of future trends. Predict which skills (both hard and soft) will be in high demand. And begin to hone your expertise in these areas. Contrary, many professionals continue to pursue learning paths that offer them momentary gratification—a quick promotion, a raise in salary and status and so on.

My invitation for you at this moment is to pause and explore whether the learning paths you're taking are preparing you to be future-ready or to stay present-safe.

Future-ready vs present-safe

Before you make any learning commitment and financial investment, such as signing up for college or any course really, pause and assess. Is this a skill or body of knowledge that will matter in the path you are pursuing 10 or 20 years down the line? There are several ways to stay current on emerging trends and opportunities in various industries and professions.

For strategic and intentional professionals, conducting comprehensive research is an action that preludes any learning decision. Unfortunately, this level of effort and commitment is elusive for many, who are still busy panicking about whether their jobs will exist or not.

If your research proves or gives you definite hints that the skills and knowledge you are considering will be irrelevant in the future, drop the idea of pursuing these. Instead, follow what will be needed then. Though you might be ten years ahead of time, history has shown that sometimes, events unfold faster than expected. This approach may necessitate self-teaching, a method not standard in traditional education and training settings. Though difficult at first, it is not impossible.

Exposing yourself to thought-leaders is another helpful tactic. Read what they are reading, learn more about the things they are pursuing and engage with them on their platforms. This type of exposure opens your mind, making you the thought-leader of your career.

When you approach your growth and expertise building from a future-ready perspective, you will never be caught off guard. Besides, you will always be a few steps ahead of others, accelerating your career growth and opening up new and exciting opportunities for you way ahead of time.

First, we invent it, and then we teach it

The more you think about the above statement, the closer you get to the fallacies of how we truly learn and why the traditional schooling system is one big fat lie.

> Want to try it? You know I love to see you play. So here you go. Spend the rest of your day trying to name just one area that became an

organised body of knowledge taught in a formal institution before being tested outside the classroom. Tricky, right?

Here are a few examples of recent events: A few years ago, there were only a few channels for mass product marketing. Print media (newspapers) and broadcast media (TV and radio) were the most common. Then the entire world of digital marketing emerged. And consequently, new career fields such as digital marketing.

Once digital marketing strategies to drive products to consumers reached critical mass, there was an urgent need to channel more labour into this space. The early adopters were, as always, quick to act. They first learned what it took to succeed in digital marketing, and then they asked, "How can this stuff be taught to more people?" This has since resulted in the proliferation of digital marketing courses.

The sector was first invented, then we figured out organised curricula to teach how it works.

Eventually, institutions of higher learning had to figure out how to integrate or rather squeeze these new fields into their existing programs. Of course, many opt for the latter. The speed at which the technological world moves is too painful for them to keep up with.

It thus makes sense that if you are pursuing a field that is evolving faster than you can blink, you are safer figuring things out through self-directed learning approaches and or apprenticeship rather than studying knowledge that will be outdated before your graduation.

I recall when the social media craze started crawling into our lives, slowly but surely. I interacted with a handful of individuals who were obsessed with the potential of these tools. And the opportunities they would create. Being not so tech-savvy then, it was hard for me to put my head around the hype.

The fool in me would sometimes think, "Hmm, how could one possibly make a living from this social media world? Shouldn't they be focusing on the upcoming tests for their bachelors?" Not that I've ever been particularly keen on tests. Once in a while, when I gathered the courage to express my doubts openly, I would be met by the same calm and confident response: "This will be one of the biggest industries in the near future, Martha".

And so it came to be that I would live to witness the rise of these same humans as influential thought leaders in the digital marketing space. That near future was not so far-fetched after all.

What can we learn from such individuals? Vision and commitment go a long way in following the less-beaten learning path. In addition, it's unlikely that you'll learn about the cutting edge in the classroom. I presume you'll get a sneak preview of it there, many years after it was invented.

Your food for thought

Do you have any clue about the predictions of your industry 10-20 years from now? If not, find out! If no predictions exist, carefully study the unfolding events and start to make intelligent guesses. In a couple of years, you will have picked up the patterns. Then, ask yourself, what tiny actions can I start today that have the potential to make me a trendsetter in my field 5, 10, 20 years from now? What do I need to learn to prepare myself to be a competitive value creator when that time comes?

You probably already know half of what you want to study

Like my friend said, "In some things, we are naturals".

The trick is, you won't know this until you immerse yourself in different experiences. Hence, why it's crucial to keep experimenting with what calls your spirit. Do this as often as you can. Constantly pivot the lessons gathered and drop what doesn't interest you or bring out the best of your expertise along the way. This way, you get to focus on acquiring knowledge and skills that are most relevant and aligned to your potential, interests, talents and aspirations.

Following the formal training path is sometimes still helpful. You acquire structure and network to navigate your world of work and collaborate effectively with others who have similar interests and knowledge. Additionally, you will be able to share your expertise with your juniors or mentees in an organised manner.

Still, before you pay that first-semester fee, I urge you to…

Apprentice your ass off

It's how our ancestors transferred knowledge and skills. Apprenticeship. Still not convinced that this could work for you? Contemplate this: Would you rather pay for college? Or invest in a successful expert in your desired industry to learn the best practices from them?

Such experiences don't fall from the clouds on a platter. We must proactively and creatively seek them. To determine what types of apprenticeship opportunities will be most beneficial to you, start by answering the following questions:

Who in my field is super skilled and a thought-leader whose approach I genuinely admire?

What 2-3 things would I love to learn and model from them?

What out-of-the-box ideas can I utilise to connect with them?

In what other creative ways can I observe their work in action?

How can I bring these learnings to my daily work?

Once, an entrepreneur I know wrote a message to a well-established thought-leader through a social media channel with two bold requests. To be his mentor and, two, create space in his company for him and a few select managers from his start-up to apprentice once a week. This would help him and his team fast track their business acumen for growth stage organisations. He received a YES to both requests!

Act on the idea of developing future proof skills

Future-proof skills and mindsets are the gems that enhance your adaptability in an agile world of work. No matter what type of work you end up pursuing, you will thrive if you have mastered most of these.

Suppose you are unsure of your level of competency in either of these. In that case, it's recommended you seek the support of a trained competency assessor. If this is not feasible for you at the moment, seek feedback from your inner and trusted circle. The people who will give you the hard and honest truth about your abilities. No sugar-coated BS. Ask them, "How have you seen me add value in the workplace and or in the world, through the skills and mindsets below, and where are my gaps in each?"

Five skills and mindsets that will remain future-proof in our world of work.

- Creative problem-solving. Because, as a species, we will continue to create new problems for ourselves, one innovation at a time).
- A high level of self–management. This is the key to hacking the remote working setup where discipline and focus are more needed than ever. In addition, managing the rising fast-changing demands and high-pressure work environments requires high levels of self-management.
- Ability to effectively and efficiently collaborate with others. This simply translates to high levels of self-awareness, active listening skills, empathy for others and the ability to shrink and dissolve the ego when needed.
- Agile adaptation. This refers to the ability to notice changing circumstances as soon as they arise and rapidly learn new behaviours, mindsets and skills in response. In doing so, one remains a relevant contributor.
- And lots of critical thinking. Oh my, we are going to need this badly. Thinking for yourself and making conscious decisions might one day be a rare gem to find.

Luckily, mastering these transcends formal learning setups. You can develop many of the above skills and mindsets by paying attention to everyday occurrences and seizing unexpected opportunities.

Furthermore, as you review this list of future-proof skills, you will notice that there aren't many formal institutions that will go deep with you in these areas. Thus, you must get creative and comfortable with learning in unusual and, of course, fun ways.

For example, a while back, I spent a couple of years organising social events. I would conceptualise themes, visualise guest experiences, execute them meticulously while playing host and having fun. Was it possible to do less and deliver mediocre experiences? Absolutely! But I knew these experiences were potentially great learning experiences. They helped me sharpen skills such as concept and experience design, hosting conversations, resourcefulness and adaptability. It turns out; these are the most valuable skills in my work today.

Learning opportunities are everywhere. Once you shift your perception of the activities you engage in daily, you will begin to spot them. Be it volunteering to organise the annual company end of year retreat, starting a social project about something that pisses you off, or making your friend's bridal shower happen.

Pro-tip 1: Nothing accelerates your self-awareness like immersing yourself in new cultures and adventures. That is why, if you are scared of travelling alone or pursuing unfamiliar experiences, you should do it.

Pro-tip 2: Your discipline and self-management skills can be developed and sustained at every single moment. Yes, by keeping up with those boring task lists, committing to 30 days of clean eating, practising 15 minutes of silence to detox from overstimulation or 30 minutes of walking every damn day.

Start small and then take on bigger challenges in your work personal pursuits. Of course, the more complex the experience, the faster you master these skills and strengthen your ability to deliver in uncertain work environments.

Account for your proven ability to learn, FAST

Your ability to learn is proven by the results you create through the new skills, mindsets and knowledge you accumulate. NOT BY YOUR CERTIFICATES!

When seeking new opportunities, future employers will need you to demonstrate how you've applied what you know to solve business challenges in real-time. They are also curious to learn how you actively keep yourself relevant and competent.

To stand out, you need concrete examples of the following questions at your fingertips:

How have the newly acquired skills and knowledge enabled you to create value in your work and overall organisation?

What problems have you solved in innovative ways as a result of acquiring new skills or knowledge?

How are you currently enhancing your skills and knowledge to stay relevant in a fast-changing world of work?

I have crossed paths with hundreds of professionals who claim to be fast learners but fail to account for it. Or others who claim to be curious about several areas, only to discover through further exploration that it's been several months or years since they touched on any of these areas. An interview conversation that demonstrates this unfolds as below.

Me: Oh, I see you've stated in your motivation letter that you are a fast learner. I'm curious what 2-3 skills or knowledge you've taught yourself in the last six months and how they've had an immediate, positive impact on your life or work?

Human: (Reluctantly, after a couple of silent seconds) Nothing comes to mind from the last six months.

Embrace the informal mentors trick

Most people think mentorship is about finding the one go-to person for the rest of your career. The truth is, this type of relationship limits your career worldview as you are exposed only to your mentor's world.

I am genuinely surprised when professionals claim they find it hard to find mentors. "Oh, I can't find a mentor", "Oh, my manager is not interested in mentoring anyone", "Where and how do I even start finding a mentor?", "How do you approach such senior people?"

When I reflect on the journeys of the several exemplary professions in my circles, there is one thing in common. They have proactively taken themselves to spaces that expose them to individuals they admire, who they can learn from, those who can challenge and inspire them for the better. They constantly seek to connect with professionals who are two or three levels more successful than them.

Over the years, they have built connections with incredible humans who have become their 'informal mentors'. Though they haven't had an official mentorship induction conversation, they set the intention to often connect, share opportunities, chat about life, dreams and challenges. Every encounter is insightful and stimulating. This is the informal mentors' trick.

This trick might also take a less physical connection approach. This works perfectly in case approaching people high up in the ranks freaks the shit out of you. Or perhaps the individuals you admire are highly inaccessible, which I still don't buy. In this case, you can commit to indulging their resources and knowledge by proactively engaging with their virtual activities.

Overall to accelerate your learning and development through this trick, commit yourself to one year of immersing yourself in the worlds of your role models and the successful experts in your industry.

Go where they go, connect genuinely with them, attend their events and training they offer, read the books they mention, volunteer in their pursuits, ask them questions when the opportunity arises, act on their guidance, thank them often, participate or engage with them in their virtual conversations, share an idea or two, and support whenever they ask for help.

While at it, don't forget to pick the gems of wisdom that emerge through these interactions and quickly turn them into actionable steps in your career.

And finally, for now, in your journey of escaping the formal learning system...

Partner with those who have successfully played the game you want to play

7+ billion of us. Surely you cannot be the only human who aspires for the things you do in your career.

If you don't know by now, you waste your time, energy, and effort listening to advise, solicited or not from people who have not made the bold moves you desire to make in your career. Stop seeking guidance from people on the sidelines or those gambling with their potential.

Such opinions though they may be well-meaning, lack the experiential and practical spice. They are untested theories. Having crowned you a scientist, you know better. So, go, find the others.

Finally, let's say you've experimented with all the ideas shared in this chapter. You feel 100% clear and confident that the best way to acquire the skills and knowledge you require to move ahead in your career is through formal education, then go for it.

By now, you will realise you only need a fraction of the formal education that you earlier intended to pursue. Thank me later.

Chapter 15

OF SACRED CAREER SPACES

It's a pity to work most of our lives while moving mindlessly and landing in places we never choose. Only to realise and regret, in the end, the time we wasted, the potential we never scratched, and the opportunities we missed. All because we never set aside time to adjust our sails, breathe, recharge and re-strategise.

An intentional career path necessitates the thoughtful creation and protection of Sacred Spaces where we can reconnect with our aspirations, remember our worth, and reimagine our careers.

The 10-year regret

"I wish someone had told me this stuff ten years ago!"

Another of those statements I have lost count of.

Every time these words escape a client's mind, I am somewhat surprised because, technically, I have, at that moment, said nothing! Yes, I have created a playground where they feel safe to explore, question and draw their learnings, and that's just it.

Hence, when one says, *"I wish someone had told me this stuff years ago"*, what they mean is *"Shit, I wish I had realised this stuff ten years ago"*.

Coming to this awareness is a sudden, groundbreaking moment. One is astonished that it took 5, 10 or 20 years for them to arrive to this moment.

Such realisations shift one's perception massively, help one discern events differently, and quickly generate new career possibilities. In this moment of incredulity, one might find it hard to comprehend that they have discovered such wisdom independently. And that is where they are wrong.

We underestimate our potential to figure things out. A powerful resource for our advancement, but one that requires us to learn to be still, welcome silence, and quiet the chatter for the wisdom to flow through us.

"How can one shut out all that noise? I always have many ideas buzzing in my head. Silence is not my thing. I need stimulation. I'm sure I need something else, but not meditation," I used to think.

Stories.

Unfortunately, these stories only kept my career revolving around the same circle. At some point, when the noise became too loud, and my dreams became even louder, I gave up and decided to immerse myself in the world of the power of silence.

I signed up for a ten day Vipassana Silent Meditation Retreat. If you're hearing this for the first time, yes, ten days of no talking, no technology, and about 10 hours of meditation every day. There are people out there who are crazy enough to do this for 30 or even 60 days every year.

Of course, everyone thought I was having a midlife crisis, or there was a big problem I was facing. Technically, I was experiencing *a potential crisis*. I believed there was more I could do, but I was not rising to the occasion.

No one, including myself, imagined I could go ten days without talking, which is why I packed a couple of bikinis as well. Just in case it was too much, I could walk away, head straight to the nearest airport and, "beach, here I come". But who was I kidding? I've never been a quitter when it comes to doing important things. So I stayed until the end.

Sitting in silence, face to face with my million thoughts, fears, unmet desires, doubts and more stories, was, yes, extremely excruciating, yet refreshing in some ways. First, it was the realisation of how much our minds are trapped in the stories and events of our day-to-day life that we miss the opportunity to unpack, make sense and consciously choose our actions. Hence, especially in our jobs, we primarily operate in a robotic mode. Over time, our careers are designed by autopilot moves. The second realisation was that five minutes of silence could sometimes feel like a lifetime of revelation, acceptance, perspective-shifting, and healing.

This retreat inspired me to create sacred spaces in various aspects of my life. Spaces where I go to reconnect, shut out the noise, review, let go, forgive and create. As a result, I emerge clear-headed and with a renewed sense of purpose. I've discovered that the more I visit my Sacred Space, the faster I achieve my goals, as each visit reveals several new insights on my way forward.

We need such spaces in our careers. Safe spaces where we allocate purposeful time to do the work of deep reflection, analysis, radical honesty, and acceptance. This helps stimulate a shift in our outlook. In these spaces, we surrender to the magic of the universe, allowing new and unexpected revelations to flow through us. When necessary, we can enlist the assistance of others to guide us—for example, seeking the support of a coach. I call these Sacred Career Spaces.

Sacred because, with dedication, such spaces lead us to an accelerated sense of connectedness with our careers and lives. Sacred because these are the most critical and defining moments in your career. They pull you out of the matrix, also known as the rat race, so that you can retreat inwards and carefully assess your progress with limited distraction. It is here that we transcend the mundane of our everyday professional obligations and chaos and rise to meet and remember our strongest desires.

Sacred Career Spaces could have saved the 52-year-old man earlier introduced from 30 years of navigating his career with ineffective and, as he shared, deceptive approaches that only led him to destinations he never wanted to go. Had he cultivated such a practice in his life, he would have noticed the omens and found various ways to adjust his sails in the direction of his dreams and desires.

When the words, 'I wish someone told me this stuff ten years ago!' form in our minds, they remind us the ying-yang of loss and freedom. Loss of time, potential, resources, and opportunities. Freedom to finally step out of our cocoons and face our careers and lives through a new lens. One of intention, well-thought-through choices, and purposeful action.

Regrettably, we go through our careers in a rush to get 'there'. We are in a hurry to get to the next big gig. We do everything we can to get there as fast as we can. Everything but creating time to honestly assess how we feel about where we are, where we are going, why we are headed there, and if that is where we want to end up in the first place.

Many of us have no idea where the 'there' they're headed to is. Other powerful external forces frequently define it. We hop from one job to another without much thought about how each truly aligns with our deepest desires. We initially delude ourselves into believing that what we desire most are high-ranking positions and higher pay. Only to realise, after so long, that they never were. We want so much more.

This blind navigation is one of the many reasons we lose our spark and settle for opportunities less than our abilities. It's a path that leads us to *tremendous but unfulfilling jobs*. It's how we forget our dreams and disconnect from our strengths. We wake up one day and realise we've arrived at the wrong place. And we have nothing else to blame but our failure to include pit stops to pause and consciously evaluate and re-orient our journeys.

If you want to move ahead differently, you must integrate these spaces into your journey as often as possible. By doing so, you invite powerful realisations into your life, putting you back on track to where you genuinely want to go. Insights that may sometimes alter your career trajectory in unimaginable ways while saving you from future regrets.

This is where you empower yourself to move from the *SCARED* (worries, seriousness, anxieties, and unmagical thoughts about your career). To the *SACRED* (connection, dedication, and reverence for your talents, desires, and expertise).

Creating Sacred Career Spaces

Regularly visiting your Sacred Career Space increases your chances of spotting your luck-dawn, noticing emerging patterns in your career, and becoming aware of your growing strengths and emerging talents. Further, you realise how your values are evolving, celebrate your achievements, identify opportunities for help, and clarify the value you offer. You connect with what you want, remember the particular desire or talents that the godmother universe placed in your heart, and everything else we've discussed so far.

In your Sacred Career Space, you reflect, connect, review, strategise, iterate, re-strategise, rejuvenate, acknowledge, let go of everything beyond your control, accept new insights and plan your next bold move, one tiny step at a time.

During your visiting hours, you are 100% focused on honestly and objectively being real with yourself. No one, including yourself, is allowed to get in the way.

You respect this time and space because you know this is the conscious path that will lead you to where you want to be. Down the line, you'd love to look back and be clear on matters such as: How did you get here? What was the thinking and intention behind your decisions? How content do you feel with the moves you made or did not make?

These spaces are both physical and mental.

Physically, you can create a dedicated corner in your house or garden. It can be under your favourite tree in a nearby forest, your cute little cafe on the other side of town, or your seaside getaway. The point is to choose a space where you feel grounded and are undistracted.

Mentally, you want to be present and in tune with yourself and your aspirations. Choose to eliminate any potential causes of unnecessary overstimulation in your holy space. Here, your peace of mind comes first. Before your visit, take time to breathe and get into your high-frequency vibes. And then repeat it as you settle into the space.

Depending on the size and timeline of one's goals, the amount of time they dedicate to this practise differs from person to person and from time to time. If you've already been practising several of the ideas in this book, perhaps a monthly practice of three to four hours is sufficient. Back this up with a quarterly or mid-year Sacred Career Space. If you are pursuing a couple of short-term goals, you may need to commit to 20-30 minutes every day until you realise your dreams. Create more time if you can. For long-term career goals, it could be an hour every other day. Choose what works for your reality and matches the effort and attention needed to realise your dreams.

With time, you will be surprised to see the momentum and enthusiasm for your goals grow, and you will yearn to visit your sacred space frequently.

Your visits become an acceleration playground. Here you define the small actions you need to take, clarify who you need to be to achieve these and deepen your connection with your aspirations.

Before you know it, you are at the top, looking down and realising that all those baby steps have brought you to your desired destination. "I can't believe I made it!" you can't help but exclaim.

And yet you can believe it! Because you did!

So go on, create your Sacred Career Spaces now!

Activities for your Sacred Career Space

When you are committed, you create time.

You can find thirty minutes, and you can find three or four hours. It's all up to you. How badly do you want what you want in your career?

Are you seeking a drastic career shift? Here are examples of activities you can include in your Career Sacred Spaces.

Paint a picture of yourself having achieved your highest career aspirations. How do you feel having achieved them?

Reflect on how your career values have evolved, and ascertain what matters more to you now.

Ask yourself over and over again: What do I really want in my career? Write everything that comes up and become aware of the patterns that emerge.

Explore what makes you tick. Reflect and journal on the type of work that brings you joy and what about it brings you joy.

Review and strategise your career goals.

Appreciate and reconnect with your strengths and achievements. Throw yourself a grand party if you want!

Edit just one section of your resume, perhaps inserting your 2-3 key accomplishments.

Update your list of achievements.

Draft a message asking for specific industry introductions and share it with five social media groups you subscribe to.

Ask a former colleague for a date to catch up on industry trends.

Reconnect with a friend who is pursuing a venture in your area of passion.

Research the latest trends that interest you in your current or future industry.

Watch a 7-minute video on how to create a vision for your career.

Read one article on successful career transition strategies and draw what's relevant to you.

Drop a message to two of your referees asking them for a coffee. Here you update them on your career progression and seek their feedback on opportunities you are pursuing.

Research top thought leaders in your industry and connect with 2-3 on social media. Go ahead and engage in some of the conversations they are driving.

Draft a message asking to be recommended to great career coaches and share it with a few relevant people.

Send invitations to connect with five recruiters focused on your industry on LinkedIn.

Research three top organisations focused on your area of interest and follow them on social media to stay updated on their opportunities.

Happy where you are? Consider these activities

Review your monthly accomplishments. What are they telling you about your potential?

Reflect on the tasks you've been enjoying lately. What do they tell you about your strengths?

What tasks have been exhausting you lately? What can you glean from this about 'finding the right job for you?'

Reflect and record the surprising feedback you received from your colleagues at the recent project closure. What conclusions do you draw from it?

Research trends in your industry for the next 10-20 years. Take one and go deep!

Dream! Dream! Dream! The sky is no limit for you. What more can you become? What unexplored potential and passions silently haunt you?

Examine your values. How aligned is your current workplace with your highest values?

Evaluate how you are creating value. Are you contributing powerfully through the particular work the godmother universe placed in your heart?

Write a newspaper article about yourself in 3 years: What will they ask you about, and what track record have you established so far?

Review your actions and career decisions so far. What could be better? How do you feel about where you'll be going?

Commitment precedes action, which precedes success

Perhaps by the time you are reading this chapter, you will feel both excited and freaked out by the long, bottomless list of ideas and actions you could take to transform your career.

Let's call this your career makeover list.

Deep down, you know these are the approaches that you've been seeking, or at least they are worth a try.

However, you hesitate to act.

Maybe you are currently unemployed and seeking new opportunities. The thought of investing so much time and effort in bringing the ideas shared in this book to life sounds ridiculous. *"Too much work", you say. "I need to focus on getting a job so I can get back to work"*. How absurd?

Or possibly you've convinced yourself such effort is unworthy. After all, employers and recruiters are all the same. So you've retreated to your shell of comfort.

Maybe you are comfortably employed, but you feel like your organisation isn't the place for you. You yearn for growth in responsibility and a challenging community of colleagues. You, on the other hand, are engaged in a tug of war with yourself. While on the one hand, your career desires scream for your attention, on the other, you've let your fears and doubts win. So you stay. Stuck in a familiar world.

Or perhaps your makeover list feels like a new list of obligations. You feel disconnected and unwilling to get moving. On some days, you experience slices of ice slowly slipping beneath your feet, freezing you into non-action.

Though you've successfully managed to buy into your own nonsensical beliefs that there is no way you can get through every one of these ideas because, well, you lack enough time, you strangely still manage to pursue other meaningless activities successfully.

Relax, friend; you are not alone.

With all the crap constantly screaming for our attention and us freely giving it away, who has time to do anything important these days?

You don't lack time or energy or the ability to put in the effort needed to act on what you've gathered so far. You lack commitment.

When one is committed, one will always find a way to get what one desires. Anything else is stories, excuses, and the fear of the unknown. Often created by the limitations, we have set for ourselves.

Can you recall a moment when you went all the way to accomplish something? Anything, really, including planning the worst party in history. Remember that sense of purpose you had to achieve your goal? That drive that enabled you to achieve the impossible no matter what?

How come such dedication is often lacking in our careers?

Take a moment right now to ask yourself, *"On a scale of 0-10, how committed am I to investing my effort and time to taking on activities that will bring change in my career?"*

If, for any reason, your commitment is doubtable (and you are smart enough to know when it is), keep this book aside; for now, deal with all that is coming in between you and your ability to commit and then come back here.

You can project the degree to which one is likely to succeed in their career by watching their commitment to taking action, no matter what.

Commitment is the fuel that moves you into action even when you are terrified that your career experiments might fail miserably.

Commitment is what keeps you working joyfully and playfully towards your dreams and goals when everyone has long retired to slumber.

Commitment is what gets you to overcome your self-created BS and reach out for help in various career areas.

Commitment keeps you ahead of the game when others are distracted by the never-ending chaos of life and instant gratification.

Commitment is the key to becoming a master of your own time and focus.

Distractions are screamed at by commitment, "I am playing the long game."

Commitment is how you gently and calmly move through the difficult phases of your career while everyone else around you throws their hands up in the air.

Once you commit, the idea that you don't have enough time to pursue every task on your bottomless career makeover list disappears into thin air.

Committed humans create time to do what matters.

Yes, sure, life will always happen, and you may lag here and there and detour at some point. With commitment, you will re-establish yourself on the right track.

Commitment is the spirit that fiercely guards your Sacred Career Spaces.

Chapter 16

FORGET EVERYTHING YOU KNOW ABOUT SEARCHING FOR A JOB

Your dream job exists, and it's eagerly waiting to meet you halfway. However, your old and familiar job search approaches are getting in your way.

To land your ideal job, adopt a proactive mindset, clarify and align your values with your career, and strategically position yourself in rich, relevant, and trusted networks. While at it, keep an open mind, so the hidden and not so obvious opportunities don't pass you by.

What is killing your dream job search game

We are all familiar with the old approaches of finding ourselves a job. For many, this includes browsing job platforms, sending tons of applications and then sitting back praying you will get a call. If it's your lucky day, the call eventually comes, you land an interview and boom! You have a new job.

But do you know how to get yourself a GREAT job, your DREAM JOB perhaps? One that is aligned with your aspirations, values and allows you to bring your best self into play?

Several reasons make the search for our dream or ideal job an elusive game. The four most common include; the lack of intentional effort, unwillingness to expose oneself to new spaces, saying yes more than one says no, and the lack of information about the nitty gritties behind the closed doors of recruiting.

Let's dig in!

Lack of intentional effort

Finding your dream job is like searching for treasure. Your dream job is the perfect golden opportunity for you to bring to full force most, if not all, of your ideas, talents and skills. It's a chance of great worth that gives you the space to thrive in ways you've always known you are capable of. To land such opportunities, you require undistracted action as you carve out your path.

This focus is crucial because you will spend most of your time in preparation mode along the journey to your dream job. Learning new skills, acquiring diverse knowledge, shifting your low-frequency mindsets to winning attitudes, leaning into spaces and networks that challenge your thinking, hanging around specific stepping stones just a little longer, and stretching out of your comfort roles by taking tasks that you probably detest but need exposure in.

When we look up to other humans who seem to enjoy and love their work while we despise ours, it's the mud-playing to get there we miss. Rarely do successful professionals share the sweat, tears and blood it takes to succeed. Hence one may be fooled into thinking a normal 'climb up the ladder', 'grinding', and 'keeping applying for the next gig' will hopefully one day get them to their ideal job. Contrary, in most cases, it's the deliberate effort and laser focus on recreating ourselves that gets us where we want to go.

Unwillingness to expose ourselves to new spaces

The networks, spaces, conversations and connections that brought you where you are will be less likely to lead you to the next level of your career and potential. You can not find that dream job while hanging out in the same career neighbourhood you are familiar with. The opportunities you are seeking lie far and beyond. Thus, it would help if you start exposing yourself to new spaces to connect with professionals doing what you aspire to do. This inspires and challenges you, gives you a sneak preview of the world you are aiming for and helps you make a guided decision if this is what you want.

Often, we are misinformed about the realities of our dream jobs. We fancy the good attributes such opportunities offer, and we ignore or are unaware of the downsides of our fantasies. I have facilitated several group coaching conversations where one individual is running away from another's dream job or organisation. It's fascinating to watch both parties' reactions as they go on and on, telling tales of 'hate & love' for the specific role or organisation.

Of course, new spaces expand your horizon and give you the advantage of casting the net wider. As we will later explore in the power of social recruiting section, growing strong, connected and diverse social and professional networks is half your search done.

Saying yes more than we say no

Let's face it. We are safer when we have a signed job deal in our pockets. This is why we say yes to opportunities, including those we are unsure of and the ones we partially like. We are afraid that if we say no, we will lose all our chances. Or we will go into the bad books of the recruiter or the organisation, thus wholly shutting ourselves out from any potential opportunities in the future. So we say yes to squandering our lives by pursuing work misaligned with our aspirations and values and allows little of our magic to come to life.

We say yes to taking up tasks that we know without a doubt will derail our productivity and performance within our current roles. We say yes to supporting our bosses and colleagues in jobs that don't bring the best out of us. We do so because we are human, afraid of being disliked and being judged.

This agreeableness gets in the way of our career pursuits. If you truly value your time and potential and are confident in your ability to create value, you are empowered to say no to opportunities that only diverge you from your goal.

We need to normalise saying no as a choice of self. It's perfectly OK to choose our worth, sanity, and potential over opportunities that only take us far from our dream careers. Saying no is an affirmation that we know what we want and are committed to getting it.

Behind the closed doors of recruiting

Finding your dream job in a highly disruptive world of work demands a great level of tactfulness and out-of-the-box thinking.

Perhaps you have met professionals who hold incredible jobs, similar to what you wish for. In seeking to learn how they landed such fantastic opportunities, their stories feel like mere luck or a collision of coincidences. But is it really?

Consider this. Many growing and entrepreneurial organisations sit on incredible ideas simply because the right human *who totally gets it* hasn't crossed their paths. For them, parking the concept is less risky than executing a vision with individuals who may not be aligned or as excited. Is this fair to the vision? Absolutely not. Is it fair to the vision bearer? Absolutely yes. Entrepreneurs and business leaders often have to choose between their sanity and the opportunities they pursue.

Hence, there exist many dormant opportunities out there that could be your potential dream job or the next best job in your career. However, unless you are preparing yourself to 'get it' by sharpening your craft, educating yourself about critical industry trends and developments, aligning these with your aspirations and proactively positioning yourself in spaces and networks where your presence might collide with the opportunity holders, you may never come across such openings simply because they aren't advertised.

In addition, often, organisations go for a long time with unfilled roles. You might in the past have applied for your dream job and, based on your research and assessment, you were a 100% perfect match. Only to see the role being re-advertised a few weeks later. This remains a hard nut to crack for many professionals. The most painful challenge for recruiters is reviewing applications of candidates whose profiles (resumes, cover letters), from afar, seem relevant, but their positioning as value creators is hugely lacking.

Over the years, I've seen all kinds of unintentional, cringeworthy positionings, from 'you called me for the interview, so you must think I deserve the job' to 'my resume says it all, so I don't have much to add.' Interestingly, this is not reserved for the inexperienced. Professionals with decades of experience also make these mistakes.

For candidates convinced that their papers speak on their behalf: You have been misled. Though the idea might hold some water in the few industries left that recruit purely based on qualifications or the names of previous employers, the truth is, there is little to no evidence of your authentic essence, your talents, personality and strategic approaches in a 2-page document. For this reason, if you meet a hiring manager or recruiter who repeatedly asks you the same question, believe me, it's not because they've run out of questions or are bad at their job; they're looking for concrete and deep substance in your responses.

To land that dream job, begin to act in ways that increase your exposure and visibility to your ideal opportunities. If what you desire is great opportunities, embody putting great effort into your search and positioning process.

Consider taking this brief assessment to determine whether your job search activities are bringing you closer to great dream opportunities or the opposite.

Does your resume include a compelling reason why you are transitioning or changing careers?

Is it clear how your skills and accomplishments might add value in a new profession or industry?

Can you recall a moment when you gave half-baked interview responses because your ego presumed the hiring manager should already know your abilities just by reading your CV?

Have you thought of approaching a career coach to help you draw out your transferable skills?

What is the size of your professional network beyond your friends, family, and work colleagues?

Are you still looking for your next opportunities on the four job sites you've known for the last five years?

I understand you are not into social media at all. But have you heard that there are several jobs shared only in closed groups?

How many copy-pasted job applications have you sent lately? Without taking even fifteen minutes to research what the organisation really needs?

How often do you customise your resume to reflect your industry's keywords, the role you are applying for, and the organisation's focus areas? If not, wonder not why your profile never gets past the first level of screening.

What conclusions can you draw from this assessment? What shifts do you need to embrace?

You are looking, but are you *really* seeing?

A few months back, I was walking along the beach. My attention was captured, partly by the endless white sand and partly by the magnificent art of kite surfing. The clear blue skies, humans happily strolling up and down, waves crashing. Everything was perfect.

For several minutes, I went on thinking, "Wow, this is so spectacularly beautiful".

After walking for a kilometre or so, I felt this strong urge to stop, stand still and be one with the sight of the kites kissing the afternoon sky. I obeyed. As soon as my heart rate merged with the calmness of the ocean, out of the blues, strange events unfolded. First, I momentarily took my eyes off the kites and instead gazed at the blue waters and the tiny boats floating nearby. A few seconds later, when I looked back up, that's when I saw it for the first time.

The picturesque of the colourful kites swaying side to side painting the afternoon with magic - and the surfers made it look so effortless! Twenty kites were flying that day, and they all looked like they were in a mystical dance in the sky.

Instantaneously and somewhat painfully, it dawned on me, "Oh my god! I now see the beauty! "I can feel the magic right now!"

All along, I had been thinking about it, looking at it, but not feeling it. This breathtaking moment would have passed, and I would have missed connecting with it as it was.

This was another of my many 'oh shit moments'. Clearly, mindfulness has different levels, and I was far off on this one.

Rock still, I stood there for another ten minutes before walking away. Few metres ahead, I offered to take photos of a stunning lady who was taking selfies. "You are stunning!" I told her and made sure I felt and channelled the impact of these words to her. She was gorgeous. I must have passed her by earlier, I thought sadly.

Taking the long route home, I walked for another hour, deeply noticing the beauty all around me, like it was the first time I was walking along this beach.

That same evening, I noticed a majestic baobab tree right next to the other one I had been staring at for days. Even though their branches were touching, I had managed to ignore the second tree. For a week, I had been living there. And for a week, I had not seen this other tree.

As I lay down under the stars, gazing at the exceptionally bright and glorious full moon that night, I made a commitment to myself *to always remember to draw my attention to the present, so I could really see and feel it.*

When one is between jobs, shifting professions, or making any other kind of career adjustments, they may get trapped by focusing on only one end goal. To quickly land their next job. As a result, one looks only at those opportunities, networks, and job boards that are familiar. With one's focus glued to the known, they risk missing unexpected opportunities that may pop right before their eyes.

The opposite of this way of being is really seeing. To move consciously through our career adventures while maintaining a laser focus on the present moment, where the gift of all possibilities exists.

A friend of mine likes to say that overstimulation will be the key cause of our demise for today's generation. It leads to missed opportunities as we are too focused on things that don't matter, consequently missing those that do. We move around the world distracted and lacking purposeful intention, and so we:

Miss the left turn, hit a ditch, and die.

Fail to hear what our partners were really trying to tell us.

Miss to notice a great career opportunity shared in one of your social media groups as you were looking at something else.

Mishear a conversation about an upcoming trend aligned with our passions and interests at a social gathering.

Fail to hear a new acquaintance at a professional networking event mention a new company in town that would be hiring for several new positions. At that moment, one was distracted by a promotional email alert.

Miss to notice upcoming opportunities within your current job or profession.

Fail to maximise the opportunities around us because we ignore or brush aside some of our talents, skills, or gifts.

We take career detours, and pit stops as hiccups and distractions to get past quickly, rather than moments to pause and assess the potential gift disguised in the misfortune. We conclude 'this is a hard opportunity to figure out', even before raising a finger to try.

We are too preoccupied with seeing ourselves as 'employees' and dealing with all of the emotional baggage that comes with the power dynamics of being employed. Hence, we miss out on the opportunity to position ourselves as value creators.

We can go on and on about how lack of attention to the events unfolding in the present moment steals our time and luck. Or we can put a pause and take a turn around.

Reflecting on some of the questions below might be a good place to get you started!

Which areas of your career need to be looking at with fresh eyes and deeper awareness?

What actions or beliefs are you currently harbouring that may impede your progress or prevent you from seeing all of the opportunities available to you?

What behaviours or actions are your source of overstimulation? What benefits do you get from engaging in these? What could you get instead if you dropped some or all of these? How would this propel you to what you really want?

What shifts need to happen in your life so you can embody deep attention and intention in the activities that mould your career?

Let your values be your guide in finding your magic and flavour

My role in India was an incredible pitstop that gave me an extended pause to explore my next steps. Having accumulated several immense work experiences across different geographies while extensively playing with my strengths, it felt right to shape the next phase of my career as an opportunity for integration.

Furthermore, it was evident that my next job would have to be a match or an advancement from my current one. I was keen on pursuing opportunities that would allow me to create value through my highly strategic and innovative approaches.

And so, from my 14th-floor cube overlooking Colaba, the mysterious old-charming bustling part of Mumbai, I created an intentional daily practice. Every end of the day, I would reflect on some or all of the below questions.

"How do I want to feel in my next job?"

"Who am I interacting with every day?"

"What do I love most about our interactions?"

"How am I spending my most magical days at work?"

"What value do I add to the world through my work?"

"What type of role will allow me to spend most of my time in the open, sometimes soaking in the sun while engaging in deep, meaningful conversations?"

Several months later, my answer was a beautiful broken record.

"Outside, lots of sunshine, mostly working at strategy level with impactful organisations. Work that allows me to be hands-on, engaging my brain, pursuing creative and innovative projects, adding incremental value, solving real life challenges, working autonomously, collaborating with outstanding individuals who are equally passionate, ambitious and driven."

Seven years later, here we are. By being committed to these values, speaking them into the world, and moving into spaces where they are appreciated has enabled me to accelerate my career to where I am today.

But before I get ahead of myself, it's worth noting that I didn't jump straight into this life.

After several cycles around the moon, I was back in Kenya. My journey of exploring new opportunities was quite familiar. I sent applications to every advertised job that was close to my background. Though I did so with my fingers crossed that someone out there would spot my application, I was equally doubtful about the various roles I was considering. Many of the job descriptions failed to capture my imagination and felt misaligned with my true essence. Nevertheless, I didn't have the luxury of staying out of work for too long. Hence I would still crawl to job assessment centres.

Despite putting my best foot forward, I wasn't as lucky to secure a job. And it was all my fault.

During the interviews, time and again, I felt something was missing - a spark of some sort. Though the roles outlined in the job descriptions seemed familiar to my previous jobs, my experiences did not connect with their world of work. I remember feeling out of touch. Thinking something in the job conversations lacked soul. I couldn't clearly articulate it to myself or anyone back then, as I thought people would think I was crazy.

Needless to say, I turned down some opportunities, and others turned me down. They couldn't get my fire, and I couldn't get their ice.

It's only after settling into work that I love, several years later, did I realise that, throughout that experience, it was my beautiful broken record that was not being played in the background. My values were the magic and flavour missing in the assessment conversations.

It's easy to dismiss values and our needs on our way up. One must compromise, we say. Still, if you land in an organisation whose setup is not a safe space for your authentic and unique strengths to come alive, your ability to thrive has been predetermined.

So go ahead and get crystal clear about your values. Perhaps you want to reflect on similar questions to those above. Or you simply want to ask yourself what the magic and flavour of your ideal job and workplace needs to be. Let the gems you find in your reflections act as your guide in exploring new opportunities. Especially if you've been 'stuck' in your current or previous career life, you want to avoid going back to the same shit hole.

When engaging with potential employers, evaluate how close or far from the mark of your ideal workplace they are. Ask the interviewing panel questions such as: what they admire most about their teams, their proudest moments in the organisation, what they love most about the culture and how the organisation supports them to bring their best selves to service. Listen to them between the lines, pay attention to their nonverbal cues, and how the mood in the room changes when you bring these questions up. These are clues to the type of organisation they are.

To thrive in your career, seeking and staying close to organisations that get your magic and are willing to fan it is vital. Such opportunities are hard to come across through traditional job search approaches. Hence, endeavour to proactively seek and move yourself to networks and spaces where individuals align with your values and magic. This increases your chances of 'accidentally' bumping into humans on similar paths and goals as yours.

As you already know, sticking to your values is one of the most demanding challenges you will face in life, especially when advancing your career. There will always be a distraction to divert your attention to what matters less or feels easier. People, often those close to you or those who have given up on their magic, will tell you that you are asking for too much. And you will nod 'YES!' affirmatively with confidence. Because you know your potential and sanity are invaluable.

Additionally, as you are constantly evolving, your values will also evolve, impacting the shape of your career at different seasons of your life. Their hierarchy will shift based on different contexts. Moreover, some of your values are likely to become limiting beliefs if not frequently evaluated, thus stalling your career progression.

Let's explore each of these ideas a little further.

Evolve: As the world evolves, so will the world of work. These changes will influence and shift your perceptions of what is essential. Thus impacting your values and belief system.

Hierarchy of values: At one moment, stability is high on your list. The next, you are hit by, among other reasons, a mid-life crisis. Suddenly you are skydiving, quitting your job without guarantee of a new one. And all those crazy things when our limits of patience are tested or hit by a robust and unforeseen wave of 'get out of your comfort zone'. In what seems like a surprise even to yourself, embracing uncertainty and taking new challenges shoots up your list, while stability falls.

Limiting beliefs: We tend to take our values as absolute truths. This works well for us until we have to move to new levels in our careers, and we realise not all the truths that brought us to our current level of success will take us to new heights. At this point, we need to let go of some of the values we hold dear to create new space for growth. Not doing so turns our values into limiting beliefs.

Let's picture this. I hold the value of constant innovation in all projects and workspaces dearly. This value also goes along well with the type of work that energises me. As a result, its importance in my day-to-day work is relatively high. In seasons when I have to bring to life a new program, this value goes a long way. However, as the program and the organisation evolve, a new need emerges. To succeed, I must start to embrace and value standardisation to facilitate efficiency and sustainability. Now, this often conflicts with innovation. Suppose I fail to appreciate the value of efficiency and optimisation and instead stay attached to the value of creation. In that case, the growth of the program and the organisation's efficiency goals will be jeopardised. In this case, one arising limiting belief could be 'I am only good when I innovate'. I believe no work output is good enough if I am not constantly bringing my creativity and innovativeness. And two, 'processes and standards will negatively influence my work experience'. This is implausible because the products will never see the light of day!

Is it possible that, despite your best efforts to carefully evaluate the opportunities you seek, you might be duped by an organisation whose practices contradict its promises? Absolutely. What I have seen in such cases is that individuals spot the danger signs within the first two to three weeks. Since one has consciously decided what environment is right for them to succeed, letting go of such an opportunity before diving too deep becomes a no brainer.

Perhaps you are already fully committed to taking only those opportunities aligned with your magic and flavour. Hence, you feel pretty happy and fulfilled where you are. What might be the next level for you? Consider what other new spaces and connections aligned with my magic you can expose yourself to. I bet you haven't met all the phenomenal humans in your field. Evaluate the new impossible opportunities such exposure could unlock for you. Review your growth curve so far, and map out new areas you need to sharpen your expertise in. Then explore the new values you need to adopt to get to the next level. In addition, where might you connect with individuals and organisations aligned to these values? Figure out and move yourself there!

An invitation to you

Think about it. How often do you sincerely think about how your values influence your career fulfilment? And if you do, do you use the insights gained as your guiding light in making conscious decisions about the opportunities you say yes or no to?

Take some time to note down your top 10 values.

Then explore further; if you were to filter your future employers based on the ideal work environment you need to thrive:

How would you show up differently for potential job conversations? What preparations would you need to partake in before taking an offer, to ensure you are carefully and critically evaluating your future employers?

How would you engage your future employers and managers during the job assessment process?

What questions would you ask? And how will you know their response is indeed a confirmation of the experience you are seeking?

What would be your non-negotiables before saying yes to any job offer? No matter how tempting it looks?

Nailing social recruitment

Social recruiting is as powerful a tool for you as it is for recruiters. Unfortunately, many professionals don't see themselves as equally important players.

You see, a recruiter's social currency (depth and breadth of social and professional contacts & social media presence) is their single most resourceful strategy for hacking hiring, fast and effectively. The stronger their social currency is, the quicker they can close roles, get paid, and move on to making more money with other projects. An almost similar logic applies for in-house organisation recruiters; the more robust the employee referral system is, the more efficient their hiring.

On the other hand, many professionals confuse social recruiting with 'knowing people who can pull strings for you to get hired', which borders unfair practices. So one holds back when they think their network is not as rich.

While some individuals may have experienced this in their journey, holding this as the ultimate definition of social recruiting is a detrimental mindset for your career.

Social recruiting is twofold. There is a technical aspect that uses social media platforms and a human network aspect. Both approaches have the same goal: connecting and building relationships that facilitate faster opportunity sharing and candidate referrals.

In this chapter, we will focus on the web that the latter is. The illustration below is a sneak preview of the powerful and interconnected role social recruiting plays in hiring.

I, a headhunter, recently connected with an incredible human at a friend's wedding. Now, this human, let's call him Glad, is a senior manager at a leading corporation and is a thought leader in the fintech industry.

Over the last two years, my C-Suite headhunting firm has been expanding our client base to include this futuristic and innovative industry.

At the wedding, Glad and I chat about various trends in the fintech industry and their impact on the future of work. We exchange phone numbers at the end of our conversation after realising we were both members of the same badminton club. We promise to call each other up for a badminton game. Party over. We part ways.

A few months go by. Though we haven't gone for a match together yet, Glad and I have connected severally through email, sharing articles of similar interests.

In the midst of all this, one of my firm's long-term clients, let's call her Bridgette, meets a CEO of a fast-growing fintech company at a networking event.

As they chit chat, the CEO shares that they are transitioning out. They are looking for the perfect successor. They are also looking for an ideal recruiter to provide thought leadership in the process.

Two weeks later, my firm was contracted. Yes, you got it right. Bridgette recommended us for the job. We put a strong proposal demonstrating our unique value proposition, and the challenge was handed over to us.

So now we have a CEO to hire, right? It turns out, Glad, my new Fintech pal whom I met at another friend's wedding, is looking for his next career move. A CEO role is at the top of his list. After several years serving in high-level commercial roles in the finance and technology sectors, Glad is ready to perform at the highest possible level in any organisation. The CEO level. He aspires this will allow him to bring his enthusiasm and passion for innovative solutions creation and his extensive skill set and knowledge into play.

Glad is an ideal badass candidate for the CEO role. He is over the moon when I reach out as he narrates how this is precisely the type of opportunity he has been seeking. He puts his best foot forward in his application and manages to emerge at the top of a highly competitive process.

This is an illustration of how social recruiting works. It's simple yet complicated. Social recruiting takes advantage of a complex network of relationships that creates a powerful & trusted referral system. This system works from the intern to the CEO level.

You will find several studies out there indicating that hiring through referrals or social recruiting, though not 100% risk-proof, is a better bet for successful hiring.

The more complex their web of connections is for recruiters, the faster it is to reach ideal job candidates. As a candidate, you increase your chances of bumping into some uncommon, not often publicised job opportunities if you are caught up in many such webs.

Get yourself caught up in the right webs

"What you are seeking is seeking you". Rumi.

To expand, your network of people who share your professional interests helps to embody your interests and be willing to move into spaces where you are likely to get entangled in their webs. Moreover, remember it's not only about being in suitable spaces but also building strong connections while there.

You are not looking for new friends. You seek like-minded individuals from different backgrounds and levels—professionals who are aligned with your aspirations or are playing in spaces of your interest. You intend to connect genuinely, share and learn from each other. You are looking for spaces and networks to inspire you to dream bigger, pursue your goals fearlessly, challenge your beliefs and what you think is possible.

If your current professional network is limited to your 4-5 current colleagues who also happen to be hanging out in the same spaces as you are, so is your exposure to new opportunities. Yes, including you, the self-proclaimed introvert. Growing your professional network is not a luxury but a necessary ingredient to further progress in your career.

Imagine losing your job and having to rely solely on the limited opportunities shared within your small network and on public job boards. Wouldn't you be frustrated?

I get it. For many of us, the idea of chit-chatting with strangers terrifies us. Hence, we put little effort into enriching our circles. This is counterproductive to the concept of social recruiting. There is no shortcut to growing your network. Your best bet is to take a strategic approach and take proactive action.

A shift in perception helps. What if you didn't regard new acquaintances as strangers but as people on the same journey as you? What if you didn't see those ice breakers as small talk but as opportunities to get to build rapport? Would you perhaps act differently?

One tweak that I have found useful in enlarging my network is to shift from thinking of 'people I must connect with', which sounds like a terrifying obligation my introverted self is not up for, to 'opportunities for learning and sharing', which are two values high on my list.

When you align networking with your values and learning goals, the drive to take action, even when scared, is much stronger. You know you are doing this for a higher purpose that feeds into your goals and dreams. In addition, if you consider yourself a high achiever, learning and sharing your expertise is part of your recipe for success. Hence, building new connections is, by default, part of the game.

Building expansive connections takes time and energy. Thus, you must ensure that you are channelling your energy purposefully and efficiently.

The table below will help you move beyond thinking of networking as merely 'meeting new individuals', but an approach that gets you to build the complete ecosystem that accelerates your growth.

The purpose of this exercise is to save you from moving blindly but strategically and in alignment with your goals.

What am I interested in learning or achieving in my career over the next few months/years?	What is everything about this area that I am unaware of? What would I love to learn to get to the next level?	What spaces do I need to move into to empower myself? Connect with who? Reconnect with who? Research about? Join which professional body? Reignite which interest? Join which community?	What can I give/share with the world? Where can I share/learn? Who needs to hear my message?
Actions for the next 3 months 1. 2. 3.			

The more diverse your social and professional circles are, the broader the opportunities you can access. A strong network increases your chances of meeting professionals pursuing exciting goals aligned to yours, recruiters whose niche is in your industry, humans building ventures you are interested in conducting your career experiments in, people looking for pro-bono services, others with numerous consulting opportunities but can't find the right partners for execution and so forth.

Once you've moved into these spaces, your new challenge is to keep the momentum going. Again, without intention and a tactful approach, your connections will soon waste away.

Someone once asked me what started as one question and then quickly spiralled into several. "How do you manage to maintain such great connections with hundreds of humans from every corner of the world?"

"Is there a country you don't know someone?"

"It must be a lot of work, right?"

"How do I keep all of these connections going?"

"You can unlock opportunities anywhere in the world!" they continued.

"As a matter of fact, it's effortless; I do very little," I replied calmly. It was and is still the truth. Though my network globally is vast, not all are my die-hard friends, yet they often seem so. The trick is to connect deeply with every individual based on common areas of interest or values. This way, we always have something exciting and inspiring to keep us glued together.

Until this moment, I hadn't paid much attention to how I built trusted and diverse connections. And how this trait has opened immense opportunities for learning, growth and personal adventures over the years. This realisation led me on a reflective journey to uncover the secret sauce behind what seemed to others like a successful approach. I am happy to share what I discovered with you.

Everything comes down to two things. What do you want? What will you do to get it?

But here is the longer story of what I found.

1) Showing up authentically from minute zero

I adore efficiency. If a day passes without a rant about inefficiencies, it's been a great day. Showing up authentically is my highest form of efficiency.

If I show up wearing a mask, I'll have to spend more time in the future either removing it or keeping it on. So, no. When I connect with new humans, I lean into showing up raw, authentic—no sugarcoating. There's no telling what I think they want to hear BS.

Do we share a vibe? Great. We don't? It was nice to cross paths.

When you show up authentically, it's faster and easier to draw those aligned to your way of being.

2) Staying authentic and building depth

Authenticity is not a one-minute performance. It requires consistency and effort, all to *build trust.*

From there, I'll continue to add depth by remaining genuinely interested in other people.

Giving them my full attention, asking about their world, appreciating what connects us, speaking and responding intentionally, listening deeply, making sure they feel heard, sharing my struggles, aspirations and all. This grows our connection and keeps our conversations evolving in exciting ways.

Be warned, though. Not all initially authentic connections last. Some will fade out. Not everyone is committed to this level of intention. It's OK if some people fall along the way. Those who follow the same path as you will stay put.

3) Distance and time are an illusion

As I write this, the date in my neighbouring country, Ethiopia, is እሑድ የካቲት 21 /2013 ከጠዋቱ 2:21.25 (Monday, June 21st 2013, 8:21.25 am). It is Sunday, February 28th 2021, 8:21.25 am in Kenya. We are almost '8 years' apart.

Ethiopia is one of the few countries that still uses its ancient calendar. Their typical year includes 13 months. A new year begins on September 11th and has 5-6 months, depending on whether it is a leap year or not. These extra days are known as 'the forgotten days,' or Pagume in Greek. I sometimes foolishly wonder if I moved to Ethiopia, would I feel 7-8 years younger? It's silly but still...

Having recognised Ethiopia's ancient and authentic culture, how does it alter how you perceive time now? Suppose you've experienced a heightened sense of flow in your work. In that case, you are familiar with the feeling of 'time just felt like it stood still' or 'went by so fast I couldn't believe I was working on this for four hours straight.' At the same time, working on tasks that conflict with your strengths can feel like a lifetime.

Time is a construct that helps us make sense of 'reality'. What about distance? With the endless technological innovations unfolding these days, you can virtually travel anywhere with the click of a button, *and feel as if you are 'actually there'.*

Monks, seekers of higher spiritual ideas such as Shamanism, have known this for as long as their existence. These humans meditate to states where they transcend time and space. Artists and all sorts of creators and innovators do it often too. You will often hear a creator tell you they honestly can't explain the last few hours. They started working on something that drew their attention so powerfully that when they finished, they couldn't remember where they were or how much time they spent on the task at hand. That's how masterpieces are born.

What's the point of it all? You choose whether time and distance will come between you and the actions required to sustain your valuable connections. If you are committed, prioritising building valuable networks and moving yourself to relevant spaces is not determined by your geographical location or how much time you have. It's a conscious choice you make every often.

You can easily find a few minutes now and then to connect, check-in, celebrate and support those in your network as a way of keeping the fire of your connection warm. You can initiate a conversation from an online post a recent acquaintance made, thus creating an opportunity to deepen your relationship. Alternatively, you can set aside time each quarter to participate in one of their virtual initiatives.

These small acts over an extended period create strong bonds. Surprisingly, this is the 'hard work' that we have forgotten or are reluctant to put our effort and energy into. It might take me roughly a week to engage my global external connections per year, assuming I stay connected with 50 humans for an average of 2 hours each. If you can binge-watch a series of 5 seasons of 22 episodes, each lasting 1 hour, you can do this.

Finally, no matter how engaged you become in your life and career, never underestimate and disregard your 'loose connections'. These are a collection of various interactions that may initially spark your interest, but it's not clear at the moment how you will take your connection to the next level.

From past colleagues to humans, you shared the same office floor with and frequent lunch chats to individuals you kept bumping into at the same networking events.

It could be the postgraduate student you shared an apartment with briefly or the retired professor you sat next to on a long flight.

The former boss, who, though you didn't click much personally, but you got along pretty well professionally.

Your high school friend's sister always shows up randomly at your high school alumni hangouts because their high school doesn't host any.

The recruiter who gave you genuine feedback for the first time in your career.

Finally, friends, remember this…

Connecting with people is not your end game

I know. I know.

It never was; it never will be. The end game is to have fun! To enjoy the process of meeting, connecting, and learning with new humans. To have fun while exposing yourself to spaces and networks that bring you closer to your career aspirations. To be inspired by new ideas and have your opinions challenged. To take yourself to the next level in your profession, holistically speaking.

Otherwise, what is the point of all this, right?

Keep your goals fresh in the back of your mind but not the key focus of every interaction. Doing so might paint you as needy and or manipulative.

When you connect with people genuinely, authentically, and intentionally, you create channels for opportunities to flow naturally. And when things flow naturally, your actions feel effortless. Your need to stay current with industry trends and be on the cutting edge of emerging career opportunities has become a byproduct rather than the goal. Which, of course, takes most of the unnecessary pressure off your shoulders. Especially if networking is 'not your thing'.

Finally, before you venture out into new circles, embark on a new hobby, or reach out to someone whose work you admire on professional platforms, ask yourself, "What am I trying to achieve here?" Revisit the table earlier shared and ensure you clarify, "What is the most effective approach to build the authentic connections that may expose me to the opportunities I seek?"

Chapter 17

WHERE DO YOU WANT TO BE IN 10 YEARS?

It's a joke, of course. Relax.

With all of the dramatic changes these days, such a question might feel awkward. Even foreseers might require assistance to respond to it.

Nevertheless, we must face the gloomy dark side of the future, explore how it influences the advancement of our careers, and what to do about it.

If you are reading this book in 2045, and everything in the world and your career is certain, I beg you to skip the chapter.

The whole future lies in uncertainty

"Putting things off is the biggest waste of life: it snatches away each day as it comes, and denies us the present by promising the future. The greatest obstacle to living is expectancy, which hangs upon tomorrow, and loses today. You are arranging what lies in Fortune's control, and abandoning what lies in yours. What are you looking at? To what goal are you straining? The whole future lies in uncertainty: live immediately". Seneca.

Honestly, it's the '*live immediately*' part of the quote that I love most. However, the backdrop goes well with the rest of this chapter. So let's dive in!

First, consider the phrase "the entire future lies in uncertainty."

A well-established businessman and friend recently paused in the middle of our conversation and shared thoughtfully (initially, I panicked he was about to give me another rant about my inexistent financial management skills). Luckily, he hit a different note. "Martha, do you realise the jobs your children will take on don't exist yet?"

Intellectually, this was nothing new. After all, it's part of my job to stay informed on such topics.

However, my heart hadn't been moved by this reality. Put kids in the mix, and I freaked out. Not about the kids, but by the thought of the world we are creating. Wondering for the 100th time if, let's say, 20-25 years from now, the world will be safe and free for our children to peacefully and confidently explore and create their own opportunities.

My thoughts spiralled further, bringing back the attention to my career. I see myself as a robust, healthy, badass, and impactful thought leader 20-25 years from now. If you are like me, such an aspiration can sometimes trigger some anxiety, knowing that no matter how much you prepare, you just never know. Immediately, my mind skyrocketed to the future, and there I was, my fit, healthy, energised, talented and ambitious self, and, wait a minute. The work I am passionate about today might also not exist then? Clearly, I was misinterpreting my friend's words, but hey! We all have our fears.

As I quickly snapped myself out of this black hole, a whisper came to me, "OK, maybe the problems you solve today might still exist (oh and I bet they will). However the approaches to creating solutions that serve that world might be different".

This brief back and forth of thoughts reminded me of the never-ending puzzle of preparing for the unknown in our careers. How might we approach our growth journeys today without getting caught up worrying about the future and, as Seneca says, losing today?

Because we do, worry a lot. Where will I be in 5, 10 years? *(Many professionals have confessed that this question terrifies them. So they simply make up their responses from what they hear from others or think the employer wants to hear).* Will I ever get that promotion? What if my boss rejects my pay increase request? Will I ever achieve what XYZ has achieved? What will my life amount to? Will my childhood dreams ever come to life? Will I ever find my dream job? Will the goals I am pursuing work out? Will I ever get a chance to show what I am really made of? What if I never get to utilise all my talents and gifts? What if I fail? These worries take up a lot of space and energy in our daily lives that we could use to progress in our careers and other aspects of our lives.

The thought of losing the gift of today and the risk of abandoning what is in my control prompted me to tweak the common career question: 'Where do you see yourself in 10 years?' to...

Where do you see yourself NOW?

...live immediately...Seneca concluded.

I love the urgency, the passion and the drive I sense within when these words roll off my tongue. The call to live immediately pushes us to evaluate what is important in our careers and focus on that. Now. If one never lives to see the future, they will have experienced fulfilment and joy in their careers along the way.

It's counterintuitive to the common idea of preparing for the future, which is why I love it. Many professionals live too much in the future (dreams, aspirations, goals and all) and the past (overthinking previous career misadventures, attached to former successes, regretting missed opportunities). In doing so, one fails to make the best use of the present moment to shape their career for the better. Moreover, one forgets that their daily actions and decisions predetermine the prosperous future they are dying to reach.

So, my friend, where do you see yourself NOW?

I often muse over what such a powerful call would propel me towards. How would I act and move through my career differently if I brought all my attention to focusing on creating and shaping my goals and aspirations at the present moment?

Could this urgent and vital urge to immerse myself in living immediately inspire me to take charge of my goals more fearlessly?

What sort of individual would I evolve to be if I decided to put a hard stop to over analysing the past and fretting about the future of my career?

Would I respond more courageously to the curious dreams that lie in my heart? Or let the tiny flames of passion hidden in the mundane of day to day light up my world of work like a wildfire?

Perhaps I would finally ditch procrastination? Or take up those new work challenges that freak the shit out of me? But must be pursued nevertheless, if I want to touch the essence of my potential?

Would I cut loose now? Not in an hour, not tomorrow, but right now, every limiting thought and the undivine ways that hold me captive?

Or do I pick up the phone right now and say yes to that incredible opportunity on the other side of the world?

Perhaps I would relentlessly pursue work that lights up my soul today? And every other day after that?

Or finally, paint by all means, even if the voices in my head say I can not? (Vincent Van Gogh). As a result, silencing them?

Would I finally step out of my comfort zone and allow myself to bask in my greatness?

The thought of ditching my stories and acting on these ideas at the present moment gives me goosebumps. The fact that I've written them down makes them feel more real, and I know that only I can stop myself from living my future today.

It's exciting to imagine myself finally taking these tiny steps. The idea of utilising my potential and living my wild aspirations, not tomorrow, but right now, in every task, in every move and everyday career decisions, is beyond thrilling.

How about you? How could this 'living immediately effect' mould how you approach your career from here on?

Take some time out to muse and journal about how you could bring this idea closer to home today.

What is on your long list of aspirations and dreams that can no longer wait to be fulfilled in the future?

In what ways have you been delaying yourself from living immediately in your career?

What activities, opportunities, tasks, and so on do you need to say no to say yes to something that will bring you closer to your highest aspirations right now?

What difficult decisions do you need to make right now to prioritise living up to your career ambitions and full potential?

And how will you feel once you've embraced this spirit of living immediately in your career? What would these new feelings enable you to achieve?

The shift from 'the job I want' to 'the work experience I desire'

Let's play with the idea that my friend and all other prophets of the future are right. There are no guarantees that many professions will continue to exist in the same form in a few years. And a plethora of new opportunities will emerge. This raises questions such as: OK, great, so what aspects of my current profession will evolve? Which occupations will be completely wiped out? Which industries and sectors will be thriving a decade from now? What new and exciting job opportunities will arise? As I write this, I recall a couple of years ago when the thought of creating a website with zero coding background would have been considered bizarre. Today, it's the reality.

Embracing these questions and the realities they present is a stepping stone towards smoother sailing in the future. Critically, it's irresponsible for one to continue to think of their career futuristically, solely from the perspective of the 'job I will be doing' or 'the profession I will be in'. Instead, one must take a comprehensive and out-of-the-box approach that prepares them to succeed, 'no matter what they end up doing'.

In this regard, first and foremost, one is to completely abandon the idea that their predecessors' approaches will help them to carve out their path to career success. If you haven't, I honestly mean stop listening to your parents' or guardians' career advice. They have good intentions, but they shaped their journeys in different realities.

Secondly, embodying a conscious approach in taking the driver's seat in matters within their control comes in handy. A great place to start is to invest in developing timeless mindsets and skills, as we've seen in the Want to Accelerate chapter. These skills and mindsets prepare a professional to be competitive, agile and capable of creating value across diverse work scenarios. Consequently, making one an influential contributor no matter what job they are engaged in.

Thirdly, one's perceptions of 'what they seek' as they advance their careers must undergo a drastic change. Many of the frustrations we experience in our professional lives result from our need for certainty to get precisely what we seek. As a result, we miss out on great opportunities that manifest in a different package. And two, we set ourselves up for disappointment when things don't go as planned. For instance, when one hopes to be a senior manager in X years in a specific industry, doing 1,2, 3. When such expectations are not met, they may feel defeated. This is rather unfortunate, given that many of the decisions that determine our career progression and fulfilment require multiple players to align and hence are beyond our control.

Getting invited to an interview? It is not always our choice. Employers choosing us over the rest of the top cream profiles? That would be the dream. Our boss being godsend or a pain in the backside? Not in our control either. Our colleagues being friendly people or backbiters? How we wish we could tell! That your job will still exist in a year's time? You never know!

Realising that the opportunities we need to partake in to express our talents, earn a living, meet our desires, bring our light to the world, contribute, create, fulfil our dreams, and achieve self-fulfilment, lie in the hands of another, can be a harsh and bitter reality to accept. It might even feel nearly impossible for us to imagine ourselves ever in the driver's seat.

The truth is, we can not get too attached to the idea of only pursuing specific jobs or professions in the future. As you explore your growth plans from here on, my invitation to you is to pause on trying to figure out your 'ideal job or the profession you will have' and instead shift your focus to 'your ideal experience in the workplace'. How will it feel to be at work every day? What interactions will make you feel happier and more fulfilled? This shifts your focus to filtering potential employers based on the experiences they provide for their employees through their culture, vision, and employer brand. With this approach, you are committing to prioritising being your very best in your interactions with coworkers, managers, and clients as a prerequisite for your career success.

You become more intentional in mapping out your strengths, talents, and future-proof skills and aligning yourself with organisations that will allow you to thrive, no matter what you are doing. When you approach your career this way, you are playing a different game. One less focused on specific industries and professions and more on bringing your full potential and talents to multiple stakeholders while ensuring you feel great at work!

In addition to broadening one's job options, this concept protects one from 'extinct professions.' One can be great at whatever they want and commit to putting their mind and energy into it. Moreover, one can rapidly evolve their career in line with the exciting changes in different industries without feeling tied down to one limiting path. Such agility gives the individual the confidence to move through their career, unafraid of where they need to be, in 5, 10 or 20 years. They know something exciting and challenging is always around the corner.

Dead-end stories that are delaying your future

Imagine you had a magic wand to create the career of your dreams. What would it look like?

Who would you need to become today to achieve these dreams in 18 months?

What kind of work experience do you need to gain to prepare for the future?

Even better, visualise yourself completing your 18-month goal in the next six months. What would you start doing differently today?

Thus far, we've adopted the mindset of experiencing our career aspirations now. We've also shifted our perceptions from 'seeking specific jobs' to 'seeking to feel our best while pursuing our work'. I am pretty sure you feel super confident and eager to move forward and start acting differently right away! And I want you to.

But before I let you go, let me leave you with a few nuggets that will help you break through the bottlenecks that will get in your way of pursuing your desires and potential in the present.

The fact is, we are destined to come across gloomy predictions that may bring us unnecessary worry—keeping us hostage from taking action. We forget that the role of forecasts is to prepare us for different scenarios. It's not definitive that all grand events will significantly influence our careers, as we've been warned. Not to mention, different countries, professions, and industries will evolve at different paces.

So what do we do in the meantime? First, as earlier shared, we can not hang around waiting for the future. "Putting things off is the greatest waste of life," Seneca says. "It snatches away each day as it comes, and denies us the present by promising the future..."

Despite the unpredictability of some of our professions, we cannot let our dreams for a better future die. Our dreams are the wings we ride on as we journey on. They push us forward against the odds. They are our flicker of hope that there is more for us than we can see with our naked eyes.

In addition, there are a couple of limiting stories that love to visit us when we commit to pursue our ambitious goals and dreams. Tuning up our awareness to catch these before they cage us from acting urgently and consciously is vital. These dead-end stories may have accumulated over the years (thus, they are deeply buried in our subconscious and have become normalised). Unknowingly, they prevent us from living boldly in our careers, the only moment that is promised now.

"When I... then I will..."

Dear friend, there is only one when that delivers on its promise of existence. It's right now. The best time to pursue those secret dreams of yours, to take those bold moves you've been flirting with all your career, is not tomorrow, not after your children achieve XYZ, not after you retire, not after you receive a salary raise, not after you finish your postgraduate, not after you have enough savings, not after you prioritise your self-care, not after you have a new boss, not after your family issues are resolved, not after your partner returns to the country, not after you make that investment. Not after anything. Only now. Now is the perfect time to start. Get up and start moving in the direction of your aspirations. They will meet you halfway.

"Oh, you see…but..."

You've probably already started this one in the middle of reading the previous dead-end story.

"Oh, but, Martha, you see...You are trying to reason with me, and I am not moved.

Excuses.

They suffocate your potential, your abilities, your gifts, your talents, your passions, your light, your wonder, your magic, your success, your everything.

Excuses often follow a great idea. They are like bugs that won't go away. No matter how much you try, "But you see..." always shows up, killing all potentially worthwhile ideas.

Excuses are the great executioners of our dreams. They squeeze the life out of them and leave you lifeless.

When I realised how frequently my load of excuses could become heavy, I resolved never to beat myself up. Instead, when they pop up, I invite them in. Sit quietly with them. And indulge in exploring what they are here to remind me of. Over the years, my excuses have become messengers for raising my level of awareness and understanding.

My excuses usually fall into one of two categories: "Martha, you're afraid of your own power (shit, what if I become successful?)." Or, "You're afraid of failure (shit, what if I fall flat on my face)?"

Either way, masked in these excuses is a new layer of fear that I must overcome to get what I want.

To gain an understanding of the hidden messages behind your excuses, pause every time a, "but you see" visits your tongue. Ask yourself, "What is this resistance teaching me about my own power? What could I be afraid of failing at?"

"I need exposure... it's hard to find..."

This is another dead-end story I love. It stems from shallow ambition, fear of putting yourself out there, and a good dose of laziness.

Often we stray further from our goals or fail to meet them because we don't mention them to the world (you never know who is listening), ask for help, or proactively and proudly share our worth.

The truth is, most of what you are seeking is accessible at one or two degrees of separation from you. OK, I made this up. Hear me out. Our world has shrunk due to the rapid increase in technological connectivity. You can agree that today, the 'I know a friend of a friend' works like magic in opening new connections.

We live in a world where unlocking opportunities has never been more accessible. Embracing this idea sparks in us more creativity, openness, and enthusiasm to seek faster, out-of-the-box ways to achieve our goals.

The many opportunities, new ideas, and ways of thinking that you seek patiently lie in the souls of humans you have yet to meet. They are out there waiting for your worlds to collide. If only you had the intention, focus, and commitment to go out there and expand your social currency.

No idea where to start? Create the opportunities yourself! You can hang around waiting for the future to surprise you with a basket full of your desires (which might never happen), or you can go out there and fill your basket!

Don't know where people in your profession or areas of interest or passion in your location hang out? Make a virtual or physical gathering, then show up and see who shows up. Maybe one person does. And that is exactly who you've been waiting to meet.

We can create our luck simply by moving ourselves towards the direction of the things we aspire. Go ahead and start doing something. Anything and everything. The hard and the easy. Initiate that conversation with a stranger in the lobby. Opportunities are hanging around in people's minds and hearts. Conversations bring them to life. And serendipity loves momentum.

Chapter 18

SETTING SHIPS ON FIRE & LEAVING DOORS OPEN

How do you discern that it's time to quit anything?

Devoting one's time and energy to familiar or comfortable jobs robs one's potential and silences their talents. With time, one 'feels stuck' in a job or workplace that they abhor.

Knowing when to set some ships on fire and when to leave the doors of specific opportunities slightly open averts blind career moves.

Discernment

How do I know it's the right time to quit my job?

Should I maintain contact with my former colleagues even if we didn't click well?

Is it time to finally call it quits and pursue that venture I have been flirting with for years?

Do I hang around for one more year so I can get a promotion, even if my boss sucks the life out of me?

Do I take this tempting offer that seems like my dream job, though it feels like a risky adventure?

Is it time for me to finally take that sabbatical?

Decisions, decisions! Big or small, they incrementally define our career destiny, level of fulfilment and success. For example, a single yes to an additional role in your job description could lead to discovering your hidden strengths and talents. The same decision could also bring your reputation as a high performer to an end if the role misaligns with your expertise and unique ways of creating value.

Because our careers play a significant role in our lives, a lot is at stake. Our source of income, our social status, our connections, our goals, our ability and need to contribute, our confidence, our self-worth, and our dreams. Even a significant chunk of our sense of security is tied to our jobs. Thus, not knowing which paths to take or which opportunities to let go of can make us feel daunted.

So, yes, it is OK to feel petrified when we find ourselves at a crossroads. The process of discernment is a lifelong adventure that can be frustrating at times. There are no guarantees as to whether the move we take will fulfil our desires or accelerate our misery. Especially on bad days, the urge to set all the ships on fire, sprinkle the ashes in the ocean and sail away on a private yacht is often too tempting. At the same time, we can't help but wonder if we are setting the wrong ship on fire.

Sometimes, making career decisions might feel like playing poker with your life. You're constantly figuring out the most brilliant move to make and sometimes taking the riskiest one. While never knowing whether you will lose or gain a fortune.

For others, making a change might feel like being stuck in a bad romance. You know when it's been several years since you first had the itch to leave a job you hate and a boss who is on a mission to shrink your light. You know too well this working relationship is not suitable for you. You will never thrive in this setup. Though you know this is bad for your wellbeing, you choose to stay. You wish they could change their ways and be the ideal workplace for you. You know they will continue to utilise only a part of your talents and skills while all your other strengths go unrecognised. And though, deep down, you know you want your gifts to come alive, you choose to suppress them. One day, you might gather the courage to write and drop that resignation letter finally. Then you remember the two things you love about this place. Choosing to ignore everything else you loathe, you hang around.

How does one break loose from this madness?

Learning to move gracefully and make conscious decisions when confronted with various career quandaries, such as: what job offers to accept, what relationships to maintain, when to quit our manipulative bosses, what upskilling opportunities are worthwhile, and so on, is a necessary skill in the dance of our careers.

The process becomes more straightforward and less burdensome when we align and connect with our values and aspirations. Stay true to playing along the strings of our potential. Learn to take ourselves less seriously. And master our nonsensical thoughts through the Magical Triple Ts approach. In addition, one must raise their awareness of the obvious traps that are likely to hold them captive from taking the decisions that are absolutely needed to get to the next level of success.

This chapter explores each of these traps, how to spot them, and the various tactics that can save you from being captured. We also discuss how to identify the opportunities that are worth leaving open doors for. Because, yes, there will be times when, for various reasons, we pass up an opportunity, but it is worth reconsidering such paths in the future.

Your signposts for change

There are two sets: The tug of war with comfort and the dream stealer 'what ifs'. Unfortunately, we entertain these traps for too long, and before we know it, that feeling of 'I am feeling stuck in my career' creeps in. And then we are stuck for real.

When you sense any of these in how you feel about your career experiences, it's a sign you are on your way to being trapped.

It's time to bring yourself into your own courtroom. And take what might feel at the moment like risky judgement calls.

The tug of war with comfort

You feel pulled in two opposite directions by equally powerful forces. You are in the middle. You are doing everything and anything possible to keep yourself safe. Unless you pick a side, you will stay right where you are.

You experience this inner tug of war when your values are unclear. Your strengths are hidden due to hanging onto roles that require so little of your true abilities. When you fail to acknowledge your actual wants. Or all three.

Without clarity on these areas (values, abilities and aspirations), one ends up settling for less, being OK with survival mode, procrastinating from making decisions, keeping up with their stories and beliefs, not believing in their badassery, entertaining fitting in and not taking chances on themselves by living by others' opinions.

These behaviours hold one back from taking the decisions that will direct their actions towards the next level of growth.

In your work life, the tug of war with comfort TV series has many episodes:

My coworkers are lovely, and working here feels like a family. I don't think I'll be able to find another team like this. (Really?)

Losing my several years of experience in this industry is a stupid thing to do. I think it is easier for me to stay in the industry I am familiar with.

I need more time before I can make such drastic changes.

Let me follow this path because it's what others or my family advocate for.

I don't think I will ever find another organisation with such an amazing culture as my current employer. (Yeah, right!)

I have everything I need; perhaps it is not worth risking it all. (Do you really? Have everything you aspire to?)

Maybe I will wait until I am a little older.

Maybe I will wait until the kids are a little older.

I want to take on more challenging and impactful work, but let me stay in my soul-sucking job because it pays more.

Take the time to evaluate any of the relevant situations mentioned above. You will realise that by not deciding to act differently, there is something else you are keeping safe, which makes you feel 'stuck.'

For instance, an individual, let's call him Gachanja. He is an accomplished individual working for a prestigious organisation. However, over the last five years, his job and work environment has turned into a hotspot for verbal abuse and manipulation. In addition, the unhealthy competition among colleagues has slowly been taking a toll on his mental and physical wellbeing.

In the same period, the itch for change has constantly been haunting him. Gachanja would love to take a year off to pursue some of his passion projects in the rural areas of his community. To boot, he has created a solid wealth cushion and thus has the luxury of leaving the job.

So why won't he leave? On further exploration with his coach, it turns out Gachanja is from a prestigious family where social status is highly regarded. Your career path is written before you are born, and it's your responsibility to uphold the family legacy. Gachanja is worried that acting the opposite will betray his family's trust and perhaps even make him an outcast in his social circles. Gachanja is caught between two opposing forces. Keeping the family's prestige and legacy or pursuing his passion. The former is the underlying reason that he is keeping him safe in his comfort zone.

For Gachanja to save himself from this trap, he will need first to address his identity and self-perception and family relations. Once he resolves his inner conflicts, he will find it easier to take the leaps to unplug from the current toxic work environment and pursue his true desires.

What about you? What are some of the underlying reasons that keep you from making the decisions you know you need to make to move forward? You know you want to act differently, but you just can't. What could you be fighting to keep safe?

Take some time to muse about a specific area in your career where change has been hard. Explore curiously to identify the hidden reasons that are holding you back. And then commit to addressing these first.

Dream stealer what-ifs

What if you lived your whole life, only to find out on your deathbed there was an alternate universe where everything you ever dreamed of in your career existed?

Wouldn't you feel cheated? I know I would!

I mean not to scare you, but rather to bring to your awareness that this is exactly what the what-ifs traps do to your career. They blind you from seeing other possibilities. What-ifs keep your world small and paralyse your ability to take action. Consequently, stealing your dreams.

What if no one had envisioned a world where we could talk to anyone at any time we wanted? What if no one had imagined a world where humans could traverse across oceans to any corner of the planet they wished to in just a few hours? What if no one had envisioned the technology that has enabled this book to reach you?

Overcoming your what-ifs enables you to move into action. You embrace the uncertainties as part of the journey, make those scary decisions anyway, and trust that you can manage the outcomes. You may be afraid, but you will do what you want to anyway.

In our careers, the what-ifs are usually beliefs we hold to be accurate, but we haven't taken a single step to investigate them and determine our truth. Or the only truth that exists. Once unchecked facts capture us, we keep ourselves away from opportunities that challenge our beliefs. Our reality is of safety and unexplored potential, and, gradually, we are stuck.

Perhaps you've come across some of these what-ifs in your journey or that of other humans in your professional circles.

What if I don't like the new industry?

What if I don't enjoy working in a foreign country?

What if I am a complete failure in this new role?

What if my manager doesn't listen to my suggestions?

What if my industry or company won't take me back?

What if I don't get good at this?

What if I can't find a job that pays me my worth?

What if this idea is not successful?

What if I don't have enough time?

What if no one likes my presentation?

What if

What if

What if

…

Snapping out of tug of wars and dream stealers what-ifs

I wish I had a magic recipe that would blow your mind here. I don't.

You should already know how your career decisions (and those you don't make) either keep you safe or rob you of your dreams. I believe that you know precisely which traps you have fallen into and what shifts you need to take.

The quickest and most effective way to reclaim your power (that never left you anyway) is to take a deep breath and decide to do so. Snap the heck out of it. Suppose you want a career change gravely enough. In that case, you will let go of your self-sabotage and limiting beliefs without hesitation.

You can choose right now to think and act the opposite of your current conditioning the next time your dream-stealers and tugs of war arise. The question is, what stops you? How badly do you want this change to manifest in your career? And why don't you get up and get moving? OK, those are three questions because I care about your career progress. I really do.

If you are entangled in a world of dream-stealers and what-ifs, working on challenging your limiting beliefs is, of course, the first and most obvious place to start. Primarily because the more you hang out with what-ifs and tugs of war, the more they become your truths. Unvalidated truths that limit you from exploring the unimaginable in your carer.

Unlocking the places where your untested truths are holding you back allows you to clarify what is most important to you. In addition, you become aware of the stories you've created from places of fear, doubt and social influence.

There are many paths you can choose to move past these. Consequently, you arrive at a state where your discernment is clear and guided by what matters most to you. Whether it's reading this book and adopting new mindsets, working through the reflective exercises with a trusted buddy, going through deep transformational journeys with a coach, a therapist or a psychologist, or immersing yourself in studying and emulating the actions of those you admire the most, there is always a place to start.

While at it, remember, these are not one-time magic wands that take away all your limiting beliefs and give you clarity overnight. Consistency and commitment to keep peeling the layers and making tiny shifts is what will keep you moving further away from the traps.

You may ask, do I need to pay for a coach or a deep transformational program? Not really, but how far has your solo trip taken you? If you want to accelerate, you need a space that challenges your thinking, helps you uncover your beliefs' hidden roots, and opens up new perspectives that untie you from your untested truths.

Designing little experiments around your what-ifs is also helpful. As we've seen in the Experiments chapter, immersing ourselves in trying out stuff is a practical approach that helps us gain new insights and understand ourselves better. In turn, it changes our outlook on the unfolding events in our careers.

Furthermore, you could keep it stupidly simple. I mean, research helps. Many career professionals are caught up in indecision and inaction simply because they lack information.

Dozens of times, I have found myself in such conversations:

Human: I don't think I will ever find an organisation with such a great work culture and commitment to their vision.

Me: Hmmm, let's see how many organisations globally are pursuing this same vision?

Human: Hmmm, I have no idea, but there must be several?

Me: OK, suppose there are several. How do you know for sure that none of these organisations has a culture that aligns with your values and is equally committed to their vision?

Human: ...

Or:

Human: I need more time before I can make drastic changes in my career.

Me: OK, and what will you be doing with your time in the meantime?

Human: Hmmm...that's a good question.

Me...

Both individuals lack sufficient information to make decisions.

Information feeds your analytical process and helps you make sound decisions. When you are informed, you are empowered to approach the events in your career consciously, holistically and proactively.

The doors worth keeping slightly open

Making career decisions requires us to judge tactfully in choosing opportunities that are most relevant and aligned to values and highest aspirations.

While we may have the intention and commitment to do so, sometimes, the opportunities presented to us may not be 100% clear. Or we may not be 100% clear if we should take particular risks at certain points in our lives. We want to, but is it the right time? Perhaps we need additional time to gather information before we make a jump. Or we need to observe how certain new connections evolve before we can commit to collaborating.

In such situations, it's OK to hold back and leave the doors slightly open, allowing you to revisit these opportunities in the future.

How do you know whether specific opportunities will matter then or not? You may consider asking yourself, "In 5 or 10 years, will I regret having closed this door completely?"

There are three possible responses. An absolute YES!, a 50/50 I am not sure as there are bits I like and those I am uncertain of, and a NO when you are 100%. The latter occurs when your values and aspirations are aligned.

An absolute YES! (but the timing is off) and a 50/50 response are the options you need to leave the doors slightly open for.

In your career, opportunities worth reconsidering in the future take various forms. There will be professional relationships with people close to your heart's calling who share your vision and aspirations. Still, you will part ways for various reasons. Such relationships are worth keeping warm. Even if, at the moment, it's unclear how you might create anything together, maintain the rapport going. One day, your worlds may finally collide, providing you with the ideal opportunity to collaborate.

Other times, you may come across job opportunities that you cannot accept due to solid personal constraints. Or it might be that the opportunity at hand is exciting. However, it demands you leave behind your current goals, which are equally thrilling and worth pursuing. Hence, you decide to focus on your current adventures.

Consider slotting some time every six months into your Career Sacred Spaces to revisit these opportunities. Check your level of interest and passion for the specific opportunity. What are your feelings and perspectives on this now? Are you as excited as you were before about this opportunity? If so, why? If not, what has changed in you? If a hint of excitement persists, and you feel slightly pulled towards experimenting, then, by all means, respond to that call!

Furthermore, if it's not the right time for you to pursue an opportunity, don't disappear from the scene as some professionals do. Yes, recruiters and hiring managers get ghosted too, and it's heartbreaking. Afraid of being written off for disappointing the opportunity givers, professionals disappear into thin air, and we never get to hear about them again.

As a society, we could do better with more honesty. If you realise during the job assessment process that you want something different, be candid in sharing where you feel you are at. And why, as much as you'd like to, you might not be able to give this opportunity the attention it deserves right now.

And then create space for an open invitation. Explore opportunities with other parties to keep connected. And set a date to sync up in the future. Creating and extending such an invitation sets you free to pursue your current goals freely without worrying that you may be missing something.

You don't know if you'll ever be immersed in these opportunities again, but you know that if your interest resurfaces, you'll have easy access to restart the conversations.

Of course, there will be times when the other party ignores your invitation. This is perfectly fine. Consider it not your luck-dawn moment.

Chapter 19

DO YOU HAVE AN ARMY OF BATTLE BUDDIES?

"Set your life on fire. Seek those who fan your flames". Rumi

Do you find yourself surrounded by incredible friends, yet in your career life, you feel alone?

Your circles catalyze who you become. It's time you began to choose who journeys with you henceforth consciously. Everything is a little easier when we surround ourselves with those who kindle our dreams, are happy to walk alongside our magnificence, fan our growth, and whose ways make us feel safe to show up as we are.

Who believes in you?

If you can count on one soul who believes in your potential and aspirations more than you believe in yourself, count yourself lucky. You deserve to be surrounded by humans who see the extraordinary in you and who inspire and challenge you as you pursue your career aspirations.

A few years ago, a stranger confided in me that her friends felt she was too ambitious. She had achieved immense success in her career, everything anyone could ask for. Why did she desire more?

It took all my strength to summon my compassion and let her know, "Honey, these are not your friends; they are dream stealers. "Drop them."

We lose too much time and energy, fanning relationships, friendships, networks, and connections that cost our potential and dreams. They hold us back from stepping into the most definitive versions of ourselves. If one is committed to pursuing the exciting goals in their heart, one must consciously choose who will journey with them.

These choices don't come easily. The path of consciousness is full of constant inner battles. Do I choose the comfort of my current circles and keep dancing with mediocrity, or do I pursue my extraordinariness at the risk of flying solo? Our humanness makes this a tough call. We are concerned that choosing ourselves and our ambitions over what doesn't serve us anymore will lead to lonely success. Initially, yes, letting go, especially of relationships we've had for so long, can be terrifying. And we'll feel isolated for a while. However, is this always the case? I beg to differ.

What we miss along the path of reinventing our connections is embodying the art of conscious letting go and the deliberate creation of new social and professional circles. To do so requires radical honesty about where we are at and what is true for us. We are to embrace our desired destinations and accept the yin and yang of personal growth.

The truth is, to get to our next level of growth, we stand to hugely benefit from the fire of those close to our wavelength—those who are committed to their growth adventures, as we are.

Once, a coach challenged me, "Martha, what are those circles you keep holding onto, yet they are poisoning your spirit, and you know it? What relationships in your life truly bore you to death, and you know you should have left a long time ago, but you stick around? Make a list of all of them."

Boy, did that exercise draw the chills from my toenails to my hair follicles! Finally, someone who believed I could fly was pushing me to the edge. This was a call for total honesty and acceptance that not everyone could stay on track anymore, no matter how much I believed in them.

I encourage you to pause and ask yourself the same question. Like me, you will feel uncomfortable, and you will find every possible justifiable story and excuse to keep some connections out of your let-go list. It will cross your mind that perhaps you are selfish for choosing to safeguard your desires and aspirations. You might even feel guilty for choosing not to betray you. This is part of the process. Keep going.

Our connections can either enslave us or inspire us to realize our ambitions. You deserve the latter. Often, along our career journeys, stuff happens, and we forget our light and our greatness. You deserve to be surrounded by humans who know and appreciate your awesomeness. And they are eager to compassionately remind you when you forget. Choose to keep moving towards spaces where your soul's calling is fueled.

But first, you will need to shed what doesn't serve you anymore. Each of us knows exactly who and what that looks like.

It's a scary process. I get it. This is why, if you are to any extent spiritual, I encourage you to consider asking the godmother universe for help. Help to get rid of everything and everyone that is not part of the big picture she envisioned for you. She never disappoints. She will move at rocket speed. You will resist. She will push back. Back and forth, you will go until you learn to surrender to the process.

And if you do, you may wake up one day and wonder: How did all these extraordinary beings who inspire, challenge, support, love, remind, acknowledge, call out my bullshit, and fan my dreams, end up at my doorstep? How did I attract such incredible humans and communities into my energy space?

You will ask this question rhetorically while deep down knowing the answer to how you got here too well.

You don't need friends; you need battle buddies

In training and everyday life, a soldier must have a buddy. A battle buddy keeps an eye on their partner. Calls them out when they are about to partake in dumb stuff. Observes any changes in their way of being. Offers help when needed and, most importantly, watches their back.

Initially, when soldiers are paired up, they are strangers. Overnight, they are expected to build an unshakable, selfless purpose and trust that guarantees they can always count on each other. It takes effort to create this level of trust, but eventually, they do.

When a soldier knows their buddy is looking out for them and fighting to keep each other alive, their confidence to keep going is boosted. Amid dangerous ambushes, this feeling is priceless. One dares to fight on despite the dangers they face because they know they are not alone.

"Oh, so I am not alone in all this?" Or, "I feel like half the weight on my shoulders has been lifted," every other professional I interact with shares. The awareness that others are going through the same craze in their careers encourages us to keep seeking better experiences.

Surprisingly, some individuals have worked for over 20 years and still feel their problems are unique. It's mind-boggling how we've managed to create such silos while we exist and operate in highly 'connected spaces'.

This solo career travelling (conscious or not) is one heck of a lonely journey that leaves us feeling even less safe. With few to non-existent trusted circles, friends, mentors or communities where we can connect, share, and empower each other through our career experiences, we are stuck with familiar networks. Thus we continue to suffocate in the masks we wear in the presence of those we've crowned as 'close to us'.

We encourage 'false friends'. Sometimes, false friends are people we spend time with but never talk about what matters to us. Sometimes it's a bitching, moaning, and whining club where we hang out and semi-honestly indulge in our dreadful jobs. Such conversations are unproductive and only dampen our spirits. At first, with false friends, we feel like we are in a community, but the reality of aloneness in a crowd returns over time.

Several people have told me, "OK, I can tell you this, but no one else because you are a career coach. I think you will understand. Martha, my job bores me to death!"

Afraid to take our masks off and desperate for a connection to numb our pain and frustrations, we spend most of our time and energy protecting our true nature from being seen or heard. We do so because our current circles don't feel safe to be in, express ourselves, ask for help, or offer support. We are afraid of being judged. Judged for our wants, fears, desires, and, like the stranger, I earlier mentioned, our lofty goals.

So we keep the masks on.

We feign enthusiasm, aliveness and pretend everything in our careers is working out just fine. Because our professional lives play a significant role in shaping our identity and self-perception (which shouldn't be the case, but hey), we fight to cover the mud. Until the mud rises, and we are sinking. Soon enough, we start to feel like a failure.

Hence, we hide.

We hide our pain. We hide our struggles. We hide our rejections. We hide our abusive working relationships. We hide our frustrations. We hide our dissatisfaction. We hide our envy. We hide our jealousy. We hide our interests. We hide our passions. We hide our aspirations. We hide our unmet goals. We hide our true desires. We hide our tears.

We hide. And then we die.

If only we had battle buddies to keep an eye on us, call us out when we were going in the wrong direction, and create safe spaces to express how we truly felt.

First, it's our interests we forsake. Then our spirits weaken. Our goals are forgotten. Our true desires are buried. Lastly, our spark is extinguished.

And then we say we are burnt out.

And indeed, we are.

The antidote - start with you

While you seek your battle buddies, are you showing up equally powerfully for yourself? Often, we are busy seeking support and cheerleading, yet we are barely pushing ourselves.

Acting this way repels our potential battle buddies. Your first step in attracting your ideal battle buddies is to be what you wish them to be for you. Simply because that is what they, too, are seeking. It's unreasonable to expect others to be what you aren't for yourself. Surrender to the fact that like attracts like.

If it's just dawned on you that your circle of influence needs a major overhaul, first, avoid the panic button. Second, commit not to entertain your current state as an excuse not to move forward.

Other times, you may need to step up and be the creator of the spaces and connections you need most. A few years back, when I coined the idea of Career Soul Sessions, I was sceptical. Could a group of strangers bravely show up, connect and share their career journeys so genuinely that everyone was moved to tears?

I knew I needed such a space for myself. A space where individuals believe in each other, remind each other of their greatness, gently challenge and hold space for each other. First, I became one who believes in self, celebrates her greatness, challenges her thinking and beliefs, calls out her bullshit, and holds space for herself, especially on the hard days. Then, I created a space that attracted like-minded souls.

It's a good moment for you to explore how you might bring these ideas into your life.

What type of battle buddies are you seeking? How are you preparing yourself to become that? If you're looking for circles of trust, honesty, genuine support, inspiration, and authentic expression, work on developing these qualities so you can attract those who share your values.

Begin to show up today like the battle buddy you need most. Those who vibe with you will spot you and eventually join you. Genuine visionaries find each other.

Do you want others to show up powerfully for you? Start showing up powerfully for yourself, especially on the most challenging days.

Do you want others to be highly enthusiastic about your goals and dreams? How excited and passionate, and excited are you about your own goals and objectives?

Do you want others, employers especially, to believe in your potential? Honey, no one will if you don't believe in yourself.

Do you want to be surrounded by inspiring humans who challenge you often? Spark the inspiration within you and share it with the world. Pursue your most challenging goals yet. Your tribe will meet you halfway.

Do you want others to recognize your strengths and talents? Become your own keenest observer and cheerleader!

Do you long to be surrounded by genuine colleagues? How genuine are your interactions with others?

Would you love your presence to be seen and felt more? How do you see others? How do you listen to them? Do you give them the gift of your complete attention, focus, presence, and genuine curiosity?

Our career journeys don't have to go on feeling unsafe, weary, and dull. We can choose to be battle buddies, first with ourselves and then with others.

Not everyone is meant to go to battle with you

OK, I know you are excited about becoming who you need to be, so you can attract your tribe of equally brilliant, supportive, genuine and authentic humans to journey with you in your career.

Hang on for a moment.

Remember to receive; you must first let go. In doing so, you create new spaces, time, and energy for building your new connections.

When my coach challenged me to audit the connections weighing me down, the shedding process was heavy. Years later, that exercise turned out to be the gift that enabled me to fly lightly and thus higher.

Some spaces and connections make professionals feel unsafe and unable to express themselves freely. There are networks you are in that make an hour feel like a daunting lifetime. Start to pay more attention to how these manifest in your various circles. My opinion? Drop them and make it all about you.

Because it is. You are reading this book because you want the best for yourself. You want to advance your career in ways that allow you to fully live your potential and see your aspirations come to life. And from where I stand, you have so much in store for yourself, so consider this exercise a long-overdue favour for yourself.

Here we go:

The naysayers

Prophets of doom

The you are too ambitious, why do you want more types

The ones who tell you, you are asking for the impossible

The ones who tell you, you are asking for too much

The ones who promise to support then turn out to be a let-down

The ones who cannot stop talking about their amazing lives, but never raise an eye of curiosity about yours

The believers of nothing will change

The preachers of this is how work and life is

Those who have given up on their dreams

The ones who have sold their souls to mediocrity

Those who say they want and deserve more but never seem to get to action

You know them. They poison your spirit. They bore you. They freeze your feet. They steal your fire.

Cut the chains already.

Yes, you will need help

We have normalized not asking for help. More so in our careers.

Afraid of being perceived as weak or fearing rejection, we condemn ourselves to figure out our career (mis) adventures, solo.

Don't take all the blame. As we have already discussed, not all spaces and connections feel safe for us to ask for help.

Nevertheless, suppose one wants to accelerate their ambitions. In that case, they must tag along with brilliant humans who are unafraid to give and receive help. Beyond finding safe spaces where sharing and connecting genuinely are the norm, another challenge we face is knowing what help to seek in the first place.

Muffled by our careers' busyness and distractions, evaluating and narrowing down to the specific problem areas in our careers is not everyone's cup of tea. If we don't know what help to ask for, we're unlikely to get it!

Luckily, you have me to hand you a cheat sheet. Let's say you are in the middle of a transition. There is a lot you need to get done so you can accelerate to the next level.

Here is a list of specific requests to get started:

Introductions to professionals from an industry you want to transition to.

Information about the management approach and work culture of the specific company you are interested in applying to.

An honest perspective on the activities you should steer away from because they don't match your talents.

Evaluation of your job search strategy to uncover hidden opportunities.

Honest and constructive feedback on your written job applications.

A 30-minute coaching conversation to sharpen your interview skills.

The fifth opinion on your profile and resume.

When the journey becomes a little too frustrating, a listening ear comes in handy.

Time to bounce ideas about a crazy move you are about to make.

When you're ready, take a moment to reflect:

In what ways do you need to evolve so that you can become the battle buddy you need? What baby steps can you take tomorrow to start that journey?

In what areas of your career would having a battle buddy be helpful?

What demons do you fear will arise when you think of cleaning up your connections? How might you get ready to address them?

What spaces and networks do you need to join to increase your chances of encountering individuals aligned with your career wavelength?

If you had all the help in the world to succeed, what would you do differently? What goals would you pursue? What is preventing you from seeking this help?

What three specific things do you require assistance with right now? And who are the three people you can turn to for help?

As you indulge in experimenting with what comes up from these guiding questions, remember that mastering your ability to ask for help is like building muscles. Keep practising.

And most importantly, this works if you are seeking help from the right people. People who are ready, willing and capable of being your equal battle buddy.

May you become one. May you meet them!

Chapter 20

YOUR AUDACIOUS PATH HENCEFORTH

Gũtiri ũkinyaga mũkinyire wa ũngi – Kikuyu Proverb

Translation: No man's gait is like the other.

Congratulations on making it here! I'd like to believe you've been experimenting with the many ideas shared in this book. You know that it is up to you to carve out your own exciting career path. A path that aligns with your true nature and aspirations.

I know, with all you've learnt, you now have the courage to embrace your gait. Walk boldly. Walk wisely. Walk blissfully.

I hope that you will never forget that you're never stuck. Every moment of unclarity or uncertainty is simply an invitation to evolve your perception so you can move to greater levels of your potential.

I hope that you will dare to bet on your limitlessness.

The world awaits your talents, magic and brilliance!

Author's Invitation To You :)

The magic of ideas is to see them in action. I am so excited thinking of you out there choosing to apply the insights from this book and start showing up differently in your career.

I am thrilled and looking forward to hearing what you've experimented on. And how that has transformed your career life.

Meanwhile, I hope you accept my invitation to join me in keeping the ideas in this book alive and sharing the gems with others.

Would you love to be part of my global Conscious Careers Connections? We are a movement of incredible humans like you, passionate and driven to create conscious career experiences. Or perhaps you'd love to immerse yourself on a deep transformational journey to reinvent your career? Maybe you'd love my presence to grace your next book club hangout?

Let's connect. I am always a social media click away!

Instagram https://www.instagram.com/omensnwolves/

For weekly magical career musings let's connect on linkedin https://bit.ly/MarthaDee

And of course, don't forget to leave us a review on Amazon. https://bit.ly/SYFSpreorder. This will go a long way in keeping the spirit and ideas alive! Thank you in advance!

Finally, I want you to know; you are never alone.

I am always here channeling the spirit of this book in every moment of your career journey!

Sending You Infinite Love & Light

Martha

Printed in Poland
by Amazon Fulfillment
Poland Sp. z o.o., Wrocław